Using Literacy to Develop Thinking Skills with Children Aged 5–7

Related titles of interest

Using Literacy to Develop Thinking Skills with Children Aged 7–11
Paula Iley
1-84312-283-9

Teaching Thinking Skills Across the Primary Curriculum
A practical approach for all abilities
Belle Wallace (ed.)
1-85346-766-9

Teaching Thinking Skills Across the Middle Years
A practical approach for children aged 9–14
Belle Wallace and Richard Bentley (eds)
1-85346-767-7

Thinking Skills and Problem-solving – an Inclusive Approach
A practical guide for teachers in primary schools
Belle Wallace, June Maker, Diana Cave and Simon Chandler
1-84312-107-7

Using History to Develop Thinking Skills at Key Stage 2
Belle Wallace and Peter Riches
1-85346-928-9

Using Science to Develop Thinking Skills at Key Stage 1
Practical resources for gifted and talented learners
Max de Boo
1-84312-150-6

Discovering and Developing Talent in Schools
An Inclusive Approach
Bette Gray-Fow
1-84312-669-9

Challenges in Primary Science
Meeting the Needs of Able Young Scientists at Key Stage 2
David Coates and Helen Wilson
1-84312-013-5

Gifted and Talented Education from A–Z
Jacquie Buttriss and Ann Callander
1-84312-256-1

Think About It!
Thinking Skills Activities for Years 3 and 4
Jacquie Buttriss and Ann Callander
1-84312-234-0

Using Literacy to Develop Thinking Skills with Children Aged 5–7

Paula Iley

 **David Fulton** Publishers

In association with
The National Association for Able Children in Education

I should very much like to thank the children and staff, past and present, of Grove C of E Primary School, Wantage, Oxfordshire and Kineton C of E Primary School, Kineton, Warwickshire in particular for their contributions to this book. Gratitude is also due to all the other schools and classes in which I have worked over the years, whose teachers and pupils have enabled me to trial and refine the ideas contained here.

David Fulton Publishers Ltd
The Chiswick Centre, 414 Chiswick High Road, London W4 5TF

www.fultonpublishers.co.uk
www.onestopeducation.co.uk

First published in Great Britain in 2005 by David Fulton Publishers.

10 9 8 7 6 5 4 3 2 1

Note: The right of Paula Iley to be identified as the author of this work has been asserted by her in accordance with the Copyright, Designs and Patents Act 1988.

Copyright © Paula Iley 2005

British Library Cataloguing in Publication Data
A catalogue record for this book is available from the British Library.

David Fulton Publishers is a division of Granada Learning Limited, part of ITV plc.

ISBN 1 84312 282 0

Typeset by RefineCatch Limited, Bungay, Suffolk
Printed and bound in Great Britain

Contents

Each of the three chapters is organised into six sections:
    Problem-solving
    Creative thinking
    Critical thinking
    Affective thinking and emotional literacy
    Questioning skills
    Case study

NACE Membership

National Association
for Able Children
in Education

NACE exists solely to support the daily work of teacher providing
for pupils with high abilities whilst enabling all pupils to flourish.

We are a large association of professionals offering a wealth of experience
in working with more able pupils. We provide advice, training and materials on
learning and teaching; leadership and management; whole school improvement;
to schools and local authorities.

We provide:
- Specialist advice and information
- The Challenge Award. A Self-Evaluation Framework for Schools & LAs
- Professional Development Courses with optional online continuing support
- Bespoke courses and guidance delivered at your premises
- Tutors to work alongside teachers in the classroom
- Major Annual and Regional Conferences
- Market-leading books for teachers
- Exciting, challenging books for able children
- Keynote speakers for special events
- Support for special projects

NACE membership gives you:
- Quick access to professional advice and resources
- Members' website
- Termly newsletters and journal articles
- Discount on courses, national conferences and seminars
- Discount on The Challenge Award Framework
- Discount on The Challenge Award Subscription Documents
- Access to a national network of members and regional groups

Founded in 1984, NACE membership includes schools, corporate bodies and individuals. Members are
teachers, headteachers, school coordinators, education advisers and officers, Ofsted inspectors,
psychologist, researchers, HMI university and college staff, school governors, parents and
educators from overseas.

Nationally NACE has regular contact with DfES, QCA, ACCAC, Ofsted, TTA, BECTA, London
Gifted & Talented and the National Academy for Gifted and Talented Youth. Internationally
NACE is affiliated to the European Council for High Ability and the World Council for
Gifted and Talented Children.

**In Partnership with Granada Learning Professional Development,
David Fulton Publishers and Rising Stars UK Ltd**

Visit - w w w . n a c e . c o . u k

or call us on - 0 1 8 6 5   8 6 1 8 7 9

Registered Charity No: 327230 - VAT No: 536 5807 26

NACE
P O Box 242
Arnolds Way
Oxford
OX2 9FR

T: **+44 (0) 1865 861879**
F: +44 (0) 1865 861880
E: info@nace.co.uk
W: www.nace.co.uk

A D V A N C I N G   T E A C H I N G : I N S P I R I N G   A B L E   L E A R N E R S   E V E R Y   D A Y

Introduction

In literacy lessons and beyond, children think a lot. So do teachers and the other adults around them. But is the thinking truly shared out? Are pupils learning to think independently, or are adults doing much of the 'thinking work' for them? Moreover, where, in our schools, is most value placed: on the product (the role-play performed, the text read, the writing completed) or on the process – what is being learnt along the way? Sometimes children assume that they have not 'worked' until there is something concrete to show for it; yet it is often in the 'stream of doing', which may precede or even supplant this end (and thinking is surely a powerful kind of doing) that learners evolve at all.

Thinking happens in any literacy-based activity. A group discussion demands that pupils reason with, and reflect on, others' views; a text being read cannot be passively absorbed, but requires 'decoding', and ought to be questioned and engaged with; and any writing task is full of choices to be made and problems to be solved. Effective teachers can plan for different degrees of challenge in these thought processes. But, we need to ask ourselves, are the pupils aware of their responsibility for these processes, or do they see themselves as mere receivers of learning (in which case, a dependency culture flourishes)?

Some teaching approaches described here will be familiar. However, this book's main aim transcends the specifics of lessons and activities: it tries to give teachers a framework for drawing out the thinking skills lurking in literacy lessons. Its organisation helps teachers to *name* the types of thinking children are using (in terms they can grasp – see pages 5–6 for suggestions). Teachers should talk about thinking *explicitly* with pupils, thus enabling them to understand their learning and, ultimately, to manage it better. (For reasons of space I urge explicit discussion here in the Introduction, and not beside every activity the book outlines, as I should have preferred!)

So what types of thinking are there?

Gardner (1993, 2000, 2001, and subsequently) suggests that people have different kinds of 'intelligence' – visual/spatial, linguistic, mathematical/logical, interpersonal (social), intrapersonal (self-sufficient), musical, physical, naturalistic, spiritual/existential – and that one or more of these predominates in all learners. The implication behind the theory is that individuals may thus favour thinking and learning in nine (or more) distinctive ways, corresponding to these types. However, learning environments such as classrooms often prohibit such multifarious and rigid differentiations of task amongst a group; moreover, surely learners should be as 'rounded' as they can be, in which case pupils notable for their 'physical intelligence' should, arguably, gain experience of 'mathematical/logical' thinking, 'intrapersonal' learners of 'interpersonal' thinking, and so on. Similarly, ongoing research into right- and left-brain thinking, and different learning styles (VAK: visual, auditory and kinaesthetic), can perhaps mislead us into narrow, exclusive practices when teaching, and may ultimately be unhelpful in suggesting a framework for teaching thinking skills.

Most writers distinguish thinking from intelligence, as well as from knowledge: de Bono (1976), for instance, believes that thinking – other than daydreaming – is the process of 'achieving a desired mental state or result'. **Bloom** (1956), in his taxonomy of educational objectives (see Figure I.1), suggests a hierarchy that distinguishes between low-level, medium-level and high-level thinking skills. Note that recall, knowledge and understanding, which may predominate in school planning documents, are skills which Bloom considers low-level, and positions at the bottom of his hierarchy! Though they are important, he believes it is what the learner *does* with them that counts.

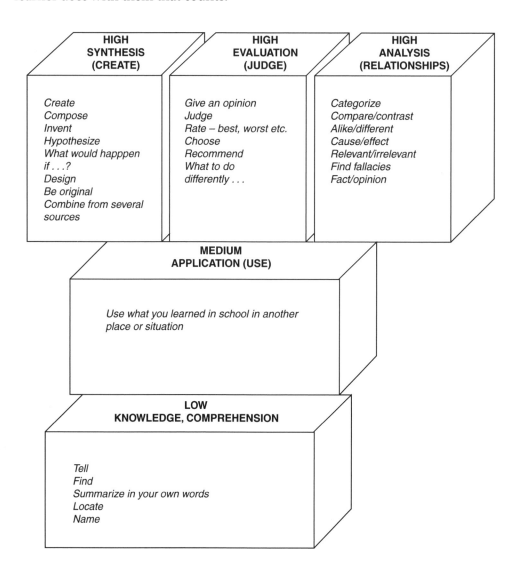

Figure I.1 Bloom's Building Blocks of Thinking

Source: From Benjamin S. Bloom, *Taxonomy of Educational Objectives*. Published by Allyn and Bacon Copyright © 1956 by Pearson Education. Adapted by permission of the publisher

Bloom gives the higher-level thinking skills of analysis, synthesis and evaluation a hierarchy too: analysis lowest, evaluation highest; in Figure I.1 here, following other writers on the subject, I do not. I do however, with others, see metacognition (thinking about one's thinking and learning), which Bloom considers an evaluative skill, to be perhaps the most challenging type of thinking that there is. Note that each set of skills, in its separate 'building block', is not discrete: during a learning experience, children may apply thinking from more than one 'set', or teachers may design an activity by combining ideas drawn from one 'set' with ideas drawn from another. Unlike Bloom, educationalists these days do not believe that a learner must progress chronologically 'from the bottom' in their thinking skills towards some 'top', but rather, fluidly 'moves' from skill to skill as the need arises; nonetheless, his categorisation is helpful.

The framework for this book also draws on **Fisher** (1990, 1995, 2003). Apart from his considerable work on philosophy for children, for which, sadly, there is no room in these pages, he describes at least three important types of thinking skill: critical, creative and problem-solving. Loosely, his notion of critical thinking is synonymous with Bloom's of evaluation (although Fisher also includes analysis in this 'skill set'); his notion of creative thinking corresponds roughly to Bloom's of synthesis.

'Problem-solving' as such is a term unused by Bloom, but it is present in much thinking skills-related literature (and is sometimes termed 'investigative thinking'). Examining Bloom's model, problem-solving seems to me to correspond to two of his skill sets combined, namely analysis *and* application: to solve a problem surely the learner must first analyse it, i.e., work out how its parts relate to the whole, etc.; thereafter s/he can set about tackling it. Bloom does not convince me that the latter process is a lower-level skill: it involves selectiveness, discrimination, calculation of risk, versatility, adaptability and more.

Both Bloom and Fisher suggest a key difference between creative thinking and problem-solving. Creative thinking is often 'thinking outside the box', or 'lateral thinking'. It is divergent, wide-ranging and not directed to one particular end: a metaphor might be the searchlight, roaming everywhere and anywhere, to my mind unjudgemental and far-seeing (though Fisher (1990) adds the critical dimension, valuing only 'creative solutions' that are also 'better solutions'). Problem-solving, I would argue, is in many ways the opposite: convergent, applied and directed to an intended goal. The more open or varied the choices (e.g. of resources or methods to use), the more creative the thinking required; the more limited, the more problem-solving the task. It is almost impossible when problem-solving to refrain from critical thinking at the same time, as the learner may often find themselves questioning whether what s/he is doing is effective and of value. The metaphor for both problem-solving and critical thinking might be a laser, probing and unravelling the detail. All three thinking modes seem to me invaluable. Sometimes learners may adopt two or three in the course of one task, at other times predominantly one. In my view, all have their uses: none is superior.

Belle **Wallace's** TASC wheel (2000, see Figure I.2) is intended to help children establish 'where they are' in the thinking and learning process at any stage of a task or block of work. (During some lesson sequences, learners may just follow some phases on the wheel, or follow them slightly out of sequence; indeed, lessons

Figure I.2   The TASC wheel (Thinking Actively in a Social way, within a meaningful Context)

Source: © Belle Wallace (2000), *Teaching the Very Able Child*, David Fulton Publishers; reproduced with permission

may become too inflexible and homogeneous if the phases are slavishly followed as shown.) Although it is often described as a problem-solving diagram, the wheel encompasses all three thinking modes, as I have outlined them. Gathering knowledge is a divergent activity, i.e., it entails creative thinking, while organising it can require problem-solving; identifying the task needs analytical skill again, i.e. problem-solving; generating ideas calls once more for divergent, creative thinking; deciding on an effective approach necessitates critical thinking and problem-solving; implementing it *is* problem-solving; evaluating work done calls on critical thinking; communicating the work may require both problem-solving and creative thinking, depending on the scope for choice allowed; and considering what has been learnt is Bloom's highest-level critical thinking, often known as metacognition.

However, there are other sets of thinking skills, beside the three already mentioned. **De Bono** (1970, 1976, 2000) divides thinking into six kinds, each signalled and encouraged in the classroom with the learner's donning of an appropriately coloured hat®:

- factual thinking (white);
- subjective thoughts and feelings (red);
- critical, logical thinking (black);
- positive, optimistic thinking (yellow);
- new thinking: alternatives, etc. (green); and
- thinking about thinking: metacognition (blue).

Some of these modes have already been covered by the three types outlined earlier; others, for example factual and logical thinking (termed by some 'reasoning skills' and 'information processing'), I suggest can be seen as part of problem-solving, at least in the context of literacy. I have therefore chosen to subsume them into that category.

Another skill set listed by many, sometimes called 'enquiry skills', is surely important enough to warrant separate treatment in this book – indeed, it is arguably one of the most crucial skill sets to tackle. Fisher (2003) and others stresses that the development of truly independent thinking skills requires the ethos of a *community of enquiry* in the classroom. Only by fostering high-level questioning skills in children, in literacy *and* across the curriculum, can teachers realistically hope to rebalance any culture of adults over-controlling over-dependent pupils, of knowledge and 'content' overwhelming skills, and the aim of some end-product dominating the continual learning process.

There is another dimension to thinking skills underplayed in most curricula for Western students. **Krathwohl** *et al.* (1965) argued that beside Bloom's cognitive, rational taxonomy published in 1956 lay an alternative, 'affective' taxonomy, based (in summary) on the degree of learners' commitment to their learning. Gardner (1993, 2000, 2001), too, as we have seen, suggests that there are learners with notable intrapersonal 'intelligences', i.e., strong powers of introspection and self-sufficiency; de Bono (1970, 1976, 2000) also promotes the importance of voicing subjective thoughts and feelings, and of optimistic thinking; Fisher sees 'affective strategies', i.e. the ability to think independently of others while taking their views into account, as a key aspect of critical thinking; while other writers list 'affective qualities', including 'learning stamina', versatility, adaptability and resourcefulness.

Currently, much is also being written about 'emotional intelligence' or 'emotional literacy': the ability to explore one's own thoughts and feelings (which coincides somewhat with the notion of metacognition, already mentioned); to empathise with the feelings and situations of others; and to help, mediate and lead, socialise and collaborate with others in a variety of settings and roles. Such ideas chime with Gardner's notion of 'interpersonal intelligence'.

This book has three chapters – Speaking and listening, Reading and Writing – covering literacy opportunities in English lessons and across the curriculum. Within these I have therefore created the following sections:

- Problem-solving (covering both analysis *and* application to tasks: with younger children you might call these aspects 'working out what we are looking at' and 'sorting things out').

- Creative thinking (you might describe this as 'opening up our minds to lots of ideas').

- Critical thinking (you could call this 'deciding what we think'). For simplicity, I have suggested approaches here that stand alone, or that can begin or end literacy tasks, rather than approaches interwoven with the other kinds of thinking listed.

- Questioning skills.

- Affective thinking and emotional literacy (you might explain these as 'thinking about people's feelings', or 'getting on by ourselves', 'with ourselves' or 'with others', depending on the task).

- Case studies: sequences of lessons described in more detail; they incorporate several of the 'skill sets' above in a three-stage format of 'plan-do-review'. This format is versatile and rich in thinking possibilities, and resembles that advocated by Wallace (2000) in her TASC wheel, and other writers such as **Eyre** (1997).

You or your school might use the five headings listed above (excluding 'plan-do-review') to audit the extent to which these thinking-skill sets are currently addressed in your planning documentation, whether just in literacy or more widely. You can then perhaps begin to redress any imbalances by injecting more 'thinking-based' activities similar to those that this book suggests.

Most approaches described in the pages that follow are deliberately general, often listing examples merely of how they might be applied to different 'literacy content'. This is intended to encourage teachers to try the ideas in as wide a variety of contexts as they can. Nearly all the activities are accompanied by suggestions on differentiation. However, beware: a thinking-skills approach to the curriculum often surprises teachers in terms of what children can achieve!

To illustrate this, below are some checklists of the behaviours of able language users. It is rare to find able learners who exhibit all of these, all the time, in every context. With this proviso, they may be useful in your school or classroom to aid identification. Note that they are generic, not age- or 'literacy-level'-related; indeed, many bullet points describe ways of thinking and 'casts of mind'. In using them to observe children, you may find yourself looking anew at learners you already know, for the effect of considering their thinking skills in any area of the curriculum is that these skills often transcend, and sometimes contradict, children's officially recognised achievements, uncovering their nascent potential instead.

Able speakers and listeners *may*:

- Show enthusiasm for, and stamina when, speaking: say more; talk about complex ideas; embroider talk with relevant illustrations, reasons or anecdotes . . .

- Get absorbed in listening or show pronounced listening behaviours: ask pertinent questions; recall accurately and in detail; build elaborately or thoughtfully on the speech of others . . .

- Use and enjoy using the metalanguage (technical terminology) of speaking and listening: 'dialogue', 'pause', 'gesture', 'interrupt', etc.

- Choose and control their speaking behaviours independently: organise their utterances appropriately; manage complex ideas or complex sentences; invite others to contribute; choose imaginative wording and phrasing; sustain an appropriate tone, register or volume; engage and sustain listeners' attention . . .

- Choose and control their listening behaviours independently: ask appropriate or insightful questions at appropriate times; produce considered responses; involve several speakers or listeners in discussion by mediating; record listening, e.g., in note form, succinctly and successfully; use responsive body language . . .

- Choose types of speaking and listening appropriate to a task, observing the 'rules' of the type chosen.

- Choose types of speaking and listening adventurously for themselves, being prepared to take risks: improvisation, interview, impersonation, unusual vocal effects . . .

- Show emotional maturity in relation to issues, themes and the 'politics' of speaking and listening.

- Be self-aware as speakers and listeners, knowing their preferences, strengths and weaknesses.

- Be self-critical, and able and willing to improve their speaking and listening skills.

Able readers *may*:

- Be enthusiastic about their reading and enjoy discussing it.

- Use and enjoy using the metalanguage of texts: 'alliteration', 'paragraph', 'italics', 'traditional tale', etc.

- Be capable of immersing themselves in texts, and of showing stamina, e.g. with challenging or 'alien' texts.

- Independently go beyond 'decoding' to take an active approach when reading, e.g.:

  - using inference and deduction (inferential skills)

  - hypothesising

  - recognising or accepting ambiguity or uncertainty, or

  - interrogating the author/text, e.g. their purpose.

- Be capable independently of seeing a 'big picture' in relation to texts, e.g.:

  - giving a detailed view supported by evidence or examples
  - collating ideas or information from several places in texts, or several texts
  - seeing the larger 'shapes' and intentions of texts
  - comparing/contrasting texts/aspects of texts, or
  - drawing on their own life experience to respond to texts.

- Empathise with points of view other than their own, e.g. the author's, a character's.
- Show emotional maturity in relation to issues and themes raised by texts.
- Be self-aware as readers, knowing their preferences, reading habits, strengths and weaknesses.
- Be self-critical, and able and willing to improve their reading, e.g. by trying unknown texts, reading strategies and techniques.

Able writers *may*:

- Be enthusiastic about their writing and enjoy discussing it.
- Use and enjoy using the metalanguage of writing: 'comma', 'layout', 'scene-setting', etc.
- Apply their reading experiences readily to their writing.
- Independently manipulate and control the audiences and purposes of their writing to good effect.
- Independently control different aspects of their writing at the same time (orchestration), even when writing at length, e.g. the organisation and layout of a text, its punctuation *and* its spelling.
- Show a love of language and an adventurousness with vocabulary and phrasing in their texts.
- Independently make appropriate choices of text forms, types, styles and approaches, observing the 'rules' of the text/approach chosen.
- Be self-aware as writers, knowing their preferences, strengths and weaknesses.
- Be self-critical, and able and willing to improve their writing by revising and proofreading.

Note that able language users may not show all these behaviours, or show them in every learning context.

Paula Iley, 2005

CHAPTER 1

Speaking and listening

Problem-solving

Speaking *is* problem-solving: speakers have to decide what to say, how to say it and, while doing so, how to respond to events going on around them, background noise and other speakers. Listening is also problem-solving: it requires listeners to make sense of incoming auditory information (including talk) and to decide how to respond – sometimes at speed. The following activities focus on the analytical, decision-making and 'puzzle-solving' aspects of speaking and listening.

Sequencing . . .

. . . in preparation for talk

If recall is involved, for example when individual children or groups are about to give instructions to someone, recount or review actual events or retell a known story, choices of sequence may be limited, but they are essential. (Sequencing becomes a 'puzzle', to be 'solved'.) If possible, ensure that photographs are available of anything actually experienced by the children (if they are retelling home or holiday news, ask them to bring in their own photos, postcards or memorabilia). In cases such as retelling a known story, have pictures, sketches or symbols to hand (or the original text, if illustrated) to remind children of the main events, or have them create such 'graphic prompts'. These separate illustrations, in whatever form, can be imported on to an interactive board, stuck to a large board, or provided to children in a set, like a deck of cards. Ensure they are in random order to start with; then invite the children, whether speaking individually or as a group/pair, to sequence them in preparation for their 'talk task', for example by dragging them around an interactive board, or sticking them in a line on to card (a 'storyboard').

Speaking on a subject, an interest or hobby does not often require *chronological* recall; however, it does need decisions to be made on a suitable order for dealing with 'sub-topics'. Therefore, when preparing, a collection of pictures, 'props' or artefacts illustrating their subject's various 'sub-topics' also aids children (for instance, illustrations of different spacecraft, of various astronauts and of several planets, if they wish to talk about their interest in space missions). Then the sequence in which speakers show these 'props' to their audience should help guide the organisation of their talks.

DIFFERENTIATION

Challenge confident children to supply more details or facts when prompted by each 'prop' or collection.

For their initial sequencing of illustrations or 'props', if it is to be chronological, ensure that children with memory problems are supported by peers with better recall. If children give talks on a non-chronological topic, especially if they are preparing individually, you may need to allocate them a helper – peer or adult – for the task of sequencing, in order to encourage debate about the reasons for their choices, and to heighten speakers' awareness that, when giving such information, there is 'no set order' for the items to be covered.

Alternatively, allow them only a limited number of 'aids'. When it comes to speaking, help the easily confused to stay on task by revealing only one picture, 'prop' or group of 'aids' on a sub-topic at a time (conceal all others in some way until they are needed).

. . . during talk

If children are recounting real events or a story, or issuing instructions, it often helps to give them 'oral prompts', or to write these up and display them as 'speaking frames' for use while talking.

- For factually based speech, or instructions with a chronological sequence, sentence starts such as 'First', 'Next', 'Then', 'After that', 'When that's done' and 'Finally' may help.

- If children are recounting news or experiences outside school, suggest 'time-based frames' such as 'In the morning', 'At about ten o'clock', 'Before lunch', 'After lunch', 'At about half past two', 'In the afternoon'; alternatively, try 'On the first day', 'The next day', 'On Thursday', 'At the end of the week', etc.

- When children are describing objects or outlining a subject, ways of beginning statements might include 'This is a/These are', 'I/We found out that', 'Did you know that?', 'Above/Below/Around/Inside/Here you can see', 'Another kind of — is', 'Another thing we/I found out about was', 'This — /These — are a bit like — because', 'This — /These — are different from — because', 'Some kinds of — are/were', etc.

- For fictionally based accounts, you might prompt speakers with 'frames' along the lines of 'There was once', '[name of character] was a', 'One day/morning/ afternoon s/he', 'The first thing that happened was', 'So s/he', 'But luckily/Sadly s/he', 'After a while/Before long', 'This time s/he', etc.

Either say these prompts out loud at appropriate stages of the children's talk, or indicate them in turn on a display board. An alternative approach in front of large groups is to ask listening children to hold up the relevant prompts on small whiteboards as they are needed. If children are talking to small groups, nominate one listening peer to point to the relevant phrases in turn, listed on a single whiteboard.

DIFFERENTIATION

More able speakers may not need the support of oral prompts; some speakers will. Encourage those who do to repeat them as you say them before completing each thought. Involve more confident speakers by asking them to help you brainstorm suitable 'sentence frames' (challenge such children either to adapt these frames when they are speaking, or to invent their own). You can also give less confident speakers smaller or shorter topics. Alternatively, break down their 'talk tasks' into more stages, for example getting them to issue only three instructions out of six in one 'cascade' session, the second three in another. Choose and brief their 'audience' carefully: listeners should be encouraging, capable of supporting them well with questions and positive feedback, e.g. signs of understanding, interest and approval.

Making choices

Giving speakers choices again highlights the decision-making aspect of talk. Brainstorm options with the children. Record these on a board or piece of paper. For instance, allow children to:

- speak *either* about a personal hobby/interest, *or* someone else's;
- present a subject they have researched *either* from TV programmes, *or* books *or* the Internet;
- show and describe *either* something they have made, *or* something they own;
- *either* explain how they made something, *or* how they did something (e.g. a game or activity they have undertaken);
- retell *either* a known story, *or* something that happened to them recently;
- read aloud *either* a fiction *or* a non-fiction text;
- give instructions *either* on something done in school *or* on something done at home;
- use *either* an object *or* a signal in group discussion, in order to indicate the wish to speak;
- *either* designate a chairperson *or* insist that everyone in a group has at least one turn at speaking/acting, to ensure participation by all;
- present ideas or findings in a group/pair *either* from notes *or* a completed table *or* from sketches; or
- agree something *either* in pairs *or* collaboratively, within a group.

DIFFERENTIATION

Give more confident speakers more choices than two. Ensure that, if they are grouped, unsure speakers are with more confident (but non-dominant) peers.

How can you manage?

Limiting children's 'speaking and listening resources' can present thought-provoking challenges. For those long-turn speakers with a tendency to ramble, for uncertain listeners or over-dominant collaborative speakers, constraints can also be a useful discipline. For instance:

- Ask them to describe or explain something, e.g. an artwork, construction or collection, without the 'prop/s'.

- When they are making up their own stories to tell, stipulate one story setting only, of the speaker's choice.

- Stipulate two or three characters maximum when they are storytelling.

- When they are retelling a story or recounting real events, insist they limit themselves to, say, the three most important or memorable incidents.

- Challenge them to describe an object without saying what it is, i.e. to devise a kind of riddle; their audience must guess.

- Insist they give instructions without touching or indicating essential equipment/materials, and without demonstrating any of the procedures (if helpful, provide them with a toy telephone at a distance from the 'doer/s' of the task, or set up a barrier between them).

- Ask children to listen to speech, e.g. a reading or an informative video, with their eyes closed, before responding to it.

- While listening to a talk, video or TV programme, forbid children to respond verbally with instant questions or reactions. Instead, invite them to draw, doodle or jot down words or phrases (e.g. on small whiteboards), or to record questions for later on.

- Forbid 'negative' utterances during group discussion/interaction, e.g. sentences beginning 'But', 'No', 'That's not fair', 'Stop', etc.

- Confine each member of a group to fulfilling one role, e.g. chairperson, scribe, doer/maker, spokesperson (who will watch the task and report back).

- Give the less dominant member of a 'talk pair' the distinct role, e.g. scribe or spokesperson.

- Give group discussion/interaction tasks a time limit.

- Constrain resources, e.g., to one pencil or page per group for recording ideas, or one reference book or computer for research amongst a number.

In all cases, encourage children to think *why* you are imposing these constraints; explain the benefits.

DIFFERENTIATION

In a mixed-ability group, some children will benefit from such constraints, some may not; this will not necessarily depend on ability (see above).

Finding shapes, finding patterns

Listening experiences have 'shapes' and 'patterns'. The notion of 'shape' describes the distinctive way in which a listening experience may be organised and sequenced, e.g. a talk may enumerate several stages of an activity, in chronological order, and a TV programme may begin and end with the same 'tag-line'. The notion of 'pattern' describes any form of repetition, e.g. the rhymes or alliteration noticed in a recited poem, a recurring pause in a sound recording, or a frequent catchphrase in a story being listened to. Of course, speakers and other 'sound producers' (singers, broadcasters, etc.) also 'break' patterns, sometimes intentionally, for effect. The following sub-categories of activity heighten children's awareness of such features. They are most successful if children listen several times: the first time for general enjoyment and understanding.

Mapping and tracking

- If children are listening to an account of a journey (on TV, recorded or 'live'), e.g. within a story or in a cross-curricular context such as geography, provide them beforehand with a pictorial map of locations mentioned. Run through them together. (For confident listeners, ensure the map includes places *not* mentioned in the account: aural 'red herrings'.) While listening, ask the children to find and number places mentioned in the order they are referred to. Afterwards, they can 'join up the dots' to indicate the route described.

- If children are listening to an account of events or changes over a period of time, e.g. within a story or in cross-curricular recounts such as the growth of a seed, supply them beforehand with a timeline of significant moments: hours, days, weeks, months, seasons or years. Again, run through these. (For confident listeners, ensure the line includes times *not* mentioned in the account: aural 'red herrings'.) While listening, ask the children to tick off the times mentioned.

- Children can undertake variants of this activity alongside any listening experience whose details you know in advance. For example, provide them with a sheet of small pictures of events, artefacts, characters or phenomena (geographical or scientific) to be mentioned by the speaker/s or reader/s. Ask the children, while listening, to tick those they heard about (ensure more confident listeners' pages include some items never mentioned).

- When children are about to listen to a short story, poem or factual account whose details you already know, tell them a few words or phrases, in random order, that you are aware they will hear. (Choose elements that are important to the content. You may wish to display these, e.g. on a board.) Ask them to listen for the order in which these are mentioned. Take feedback on this afterwards.

DIFFERENTIATION

Give able listeners more, uncertain listeners fewer features to listen out for. Get the latter to work with partners who concentrate well.

Comparing and contrasting

- Use a listening context in which several people or things are described, for example a programme about castles, or a talk about several features of life 'then and now'. Ask listeners to spot as many differences and similarities as they can, e.g. in the way different castles were built, who used them and how; or in nineteenth- and twenty-first-century forms of transport. Collect feedback afterwards. You can invite children to contribute labelled drawings for classroom posters, deciding whether these should be stuck in the 'Same' or 'Different' columns.

- After any listening experience in which events are recounted, e.g. a play, a story or news retold, present children with a short list, or pictures representing, these events. Ask them to distinguish major incidents from minor. Encourage debate; children must justify their views.

DIFFERENTIATION

Able listeners participating in any comparing/constrasting activity can be challenged to listen only once; uncertain listeners may benefit from listening again (if possible, record any talk, dramatic scene or reading so that you can replay it). They will also need shorter listening experiences. Alternatively, interrupt their listening at regular intervals, questioning them to ensure that they are 'still on listening task'.

Solving puzzles, using clues

There are puzzles in much of what we listen to: some with definite 'answers', some without. The sub-categories of puzzle-solving activity below illustrate this.

Information gap

In stories told or read, or in enacted dramas, instead of being told characters' feelings and motivations, or having events explained in detail, children are often invited to work things out for themselves. Be alert to listening contexts in which such 'information gaps' are there for children to explore. For instance, it may be possible to ask:

- How did the character/s feel? (If feelings are betrayed only by actions or tone of voice.)

- Why did the character/s behave, or events happen, as they did?

- Who is/was it? (If a change, action, noise, etc. is described without attributing it for definite to one character.)

- How did the character/s do that? (If a problem or solution is narrated without a detailed explanation of how it happened.)

Ask children to justify their answers with evidence from their listening.

Guessing games

For example:

- 'Turn down the sound' occasionally while children are listening to a recording, programme, talk or reading (if someone is speaking, they should mouth silently). Invite children to guess which words or phrases have been missed. They should tell you which words they heard just before and after the silence, to help justify their ideas (for instance, 'I knew the missing words were "who lived in a" because the word before was "bear" and the word after was "forest" ').

- Read or say two (or more) sentences and invite children to tell you where a certain punctuation mark should be, e.g. a full stop, exclamation or question mark, comma or speech marks. They should 'race' to put their hands up at the appropriate moments (alternatively, they can raise punctuation cards, e.g. on 'punctuation fans', if available); ask them to tell you the words they think they heard immediately before and after the punctuation. Again, they must justify their answers, for instance, 'I knew the full stop went there because the word "water" finished off the first idea you read us'.

Exploring dilemmas

Ensure that some of the children's opportunities for listening, and for drama, present them with dilemmas to explore. Many stories, real-life reminiscences, narrative poems and texts for enactment describe characters in difficult or decision-making situations. Seek out such common scenarios as:

- deciding what to wear for particular weather, a particular season or occasion;
- deciding whom to invite to something;
- trying to resolve conflict or an argument, e.g. in the playground;
- not knowing whether to tell the truth;
- being unsure how to say sorry;

- deciding what to wish for (e.g., if given a magic wish);
- needing to cross something wide, climb something high or bypass something dangerous;
- thinking what to do in a frightening situation; or
- choosing a limited number of things to take on a journey.

Get the children to listen to and/or watch the dilemma as it unfolds (whether through a reading, a TV programme, a video recording or some kind of drama). Stop it before a solution is reached. Invite the children to explore the problem for themselves through discussion or role play, considering what they would do and why.

A further 'dilemma' automatically occurs whenever children undertake work that is intended to be collaborative, i.e. with the aim of a joint outcome. How can children manage their group discussion/interaction to ensure participation by all without some children emerging as dominant? Ask them, while engaged in a suitable collaborative task, to devise a set of tips or rules that help make it successful.

After feedback, celebrate the children's most practical, thoughtful and appropriate ideas, e.g. by asking them to rehearse and re-enact a short scene in front of others or to do an illustrated poster of advice.

DIFFERENTIATION

Get confident thinkers to respond unaided; support unconfident thinkers by suggesting a few scenarios or solutions. Some should be feasible, some should not 'fit' the context and some should be unworkable. Encourage them to criticise and select from your examples.

Creative thinking

Odd one out

Do this when inviting a child to talk to a group or the class, e.g. recounting news, recent events or a recent activity, or summarising a known story. Ask him/her to limit the talk to three events, and details of those events. Brief him/her privately to invent one of them, adding enough detail to make it sound convincing. The aim is to outwit the audience, i.e. for them not to suspect or notice. (Of course this 'game' also promotes sharp listening skills!)

DIFFERENTIATION

Confident children can devise their talk independently; diffident children may benefit from rehearsing their three events with a trusted partner or adult. Before their talk the latter may need discussion to establish what is meant by 'events'. Rather than giving them free choice, you might even suggest just two fictional events to choose between, and the kinds of embellishments that will make either account seem convincing to listeners.

How many ways can you describe . . .?

This is another activity suited to a talk by one speaker to a group or the class. Give the child an object that has plenty of detail, e.g. a decorated container, an elaborate piece of clothing, an intricate tool or a detailed picture. Challenge them to describe it as fully as possible, i.e. to make a wide variety of different statements about it. If desired, the audience can keep a tally of the number of statements made, or you can time the talk to see how long the child is able to sustain the description. Several children might compete in one session to see who can describe the object in most detail, or for longest.

DIFFERENTIATION

Able speakers will be confident enough to begin their sentences unaided; 'speaking frames' can help less confident speakers, whether displayed on a poster or board, or suggested by an adult as the talk proceeds, for example:

- 'When I first saw this, I thought it was . . .'
- 'It has . . .'
- 'On/under/inside/above/around/near [fill in the blank], there is . . .'
- 'There is/are . . .'
- 'Someone has [fill in the blank: what someone has done to the object]'
- 'Maybe this is for/about . . .'

Design your own . . .

If you wish a child or group to do a talk or presentation on a subject, suggest that they design a format for it. Urge them to try the unusual, and yet be informative. Ideas might include:

- Role-play as if they are participants in a programme on TV, e.g., a commentator, an interviewer and interviewee, or a discussion panel.
- Mime.
- A short play, e.g. a puppet play, acting out events or conveying facts.
- Graphic storyboards, held up in sequence.
- A demonstration, e.g. of a model or collection.

DIFFERENTIATION

Free choice may suit more adventurous children; with others, give them a limited range of options, e.g. two from the above list. For those who find organisation difficult, you may need to help them plan and timetable any work involved in preparation, and to monitor their progress closely.

Story build-up

This activity encourages creative thinking while both speaking and listening. Begin storytelling with one word, seated in a group or whole-class circle. Ask children to add a word at a time, in order, round the circle. For example, the teacher might begin with 'Far', the next child might add 'far', the next 'away', and succeeding children 'there', 'lived', 'a' and 'king'. Allow shy or unconfident children to stay silent if they are unsure what to add; after a few turns of the circle, many will gain in confidence and begin to contribute. Only 'edit' children's narration to the extent of querying ideas that are ungrammatical or not expressed in whole sentences, and new ideas for the story that no longer 'fit' details that have already been included. Ideally, continue until the story is finished (at a certain point, you may need to warn children of the need to start to bring it to a close, but allow them several whole sentences, i.e. probably at least two 'turns' of the circle, in which to do this).

DIFFERENTIATION

A variant is suitable for more adventurous children. Every time someone introduces a noun (e.g. 'king', 'mountain', 'pirates') or adjective (e.g. 'scary', 'sharp', 'beautiful', 'red') to the narrative, 'stop the clock' in some way, e.g. with a bell, and ask everyone in the group to brainstorm two or three alternatives to that suggested. A vote should then be taken on the favourite, and the winning word inserted in the story so that it can continue.

You may help an inhibited group by placing a large sheet of paper in the centre of the circle. The teacher should begin by drawing a shape or object on it in crayon, e.g. a pointed shape, before suggesting a sentence that might plausibly accompany it, e.g. 'Far far away there was a mountain.' Invite each child in turn to add to your drawing, and then to invent a sentence (not a word) that plausibly accompanies it; for example, if they added a circle to the 'mountain' they might say, 'It had an eye to watch the land around it', or 'On the top was a round rock made of solid gold.' Children continue in this way, their drawings helping to suggest new ideas. At the end, a copy of the 'drawing' can be exhibited alongside a written record of the story, which the teacher may scribe or tape-record as the storytelling progresses.

Memory jogger

This is a useful listening practice, while stimulating children's use of varied vocabulary. Undertake it having watched any video or TV programme with the children. Ensure that you are familiar with the recording, and have written yourself a summary of its content. Explain to children beforehand that afterwards, they are going to help you recall the video or programme. After watching, read out your summary. Stop every so often, omitting key nouns or adjectives, for example, 'They did not have washing machines in [blank] times' (answer: Victorian), or 'Some people worship in [blank], other people worship in [blank]' (answers: churches and temples). Encourage children to suggest *as many words as they can* that 'fit' your blanks appropriately. Celebrate the variety of their answers, stressing that there is no 'wrong' answer as long as it is appropriate (e.g., 'olden', 'nineteenth-century' and 'our great-great-grandparents'' might all fit the 'blank' before 'times').

DIFFERENTIATION

Do not guide your most confident listeners. Give children who find this difficult a choice of alternatives for each 'blank' you leave in your summary. Some should be appropriate, some should be red herrings, e.g. 'Tudor' and 'parents'' as well as 'Victorian' and 'great-great-grandparents'' in the example above. Encourage them to identify *all* the words that might fit your 'blanks'.

Sharing shared talk

This activity is useful for summative or formative assessment after a significant period of using, and discussing the etiquette of, collaborative talk in class.

Ask children, in groups or pairs, to find a way of showing what they have learnt so far about:

- sharing out talk in a group; and
- dealing with disagreements.

They must design a way of presenting this to others. You might give them optional formats, such as:

- a poster;
- a mini-lesson, 'teacher style';
- role-play, perhaps with a commentator;
- small world play or play with soft toys or puppets, in role; or
- contrasting pictures, explaining features of unsuccessful and successful talk in speech bubbles and labelling.

DIFFERENTIATION

Give adventurous children free choice of format, listing the ideas above as examples only; give less confident children a more limited choice.

Same words, different meaning

This drama activity encourages children to use their vocal range and body language as creatively as they can. Give them a simple sentence, e.g. 'The cat sat on the mat.' Invite them to deliver this line to a partner in as many ways as possible, each time expressing a different emotion, e.g. angrily, fearfully, shyly, happily, sadly, anxiously, excitedly, drearily, proudly, slyly, secretively. Ask partners to react as they think appropriate when they see their peers' behaviour, e.g. by running away, offering comfort, etc.; or else to guess what emotion is being shown. After each different rendering, as a whole group review the body language and vocal features that accompanied it (e.g. clenched fists, gritted teeth, growliness, loudness). You might wish to record the children's observations in some form, e.g. labelled stick-figure sketches of each emotion.

> ### DIFFERENTIATION
>
> Leave assured children to choose their own emotions; give less confident children ideas for some emotions to get them started.

Pretend you are . . .

This drama activity can incorporate word-level work that the children are undertaking in literacy. For instance, ask them (in groups or pairs) to think of people, animals, plants, places, objects, activities or imaginary beings:

- that begin with a particular letter or sound, e.g. 'c' or the /*ch*/ sound;
- that include particular letters or sounds, e.g. 'gh' or the long /*ie*/ sound;
- that are two syllables long (or three); or
- that share a rhyme, e.g. —at or the /*air*/ sound.

Brief them to improvise, then practise brief role-plays or mimes involving these. They may benefit from dressing up or using 'props'. Ideally, there should be some element of story in their dramatisation, i.e., they should not just 'act out what they represent'. If desired, they can then perform their scenarios for an audience, e.g. the rest of their group or class. An option is to challenge other children to suggest what letter, sound or number of syllables they have featured in their dramas.

> ### DIFFERENTIATION
>
> Give confident children free choice, unconfident children a limited range of options, e.g. for the letter 'c', a cat, a car or a captain; however, with all children it can be revealing to suggest a few 'red herrings', e.g. in this case a kitchen and a kite. Those unsure about group role-play may benefit from simply acting out their choice individually through mime, charades-style.

Critical thinking

Many of the activities described below can follow, or be incorporated into, many of those described in the 'Problem-solving' and 'Creative thinking' sections of this chapter. Most can equally stand alone.

Rating and choosing

Immediately after a listening experience, or their participation in talk, ask children to identify and rate (for example as first, second and third):

- the 'best' events, characters, settings, facts or descriptions from what they were listening to;
- from a story or poem read to them, the 'top' phonemes – perhaps on the basis of how often they noticed them, or on which they liked best;
- the 'top' speakers, characters or participants, e.g. in a talk, group discussion, performance, TV programme or video;
- the 'best' or most memorable words, phrases, lines, sentences, suggestions or pieces of dialogue they heard or participated in during talk, a performance or video;
- the 'top' listening or speaking experiences recently encountered;
- the 'best', funniest, most unusual, etc. stories or poems read aloud to them; or
- their favourite kinds of listening or talk experience.

They can agree this 'ranking' through discussion in a group, or decide it individually. Ask them to justify their preferences.

In further variants of this task:

- Ask children to invent three titles for a performance, programme or video watched, or a reading listened to, whose original title you have concealed. Alternatively, ask them to give three possible titles to a piece of drama they have performed. Afterwards ask them to rank these as their first, second and third favourites and to justify why.
- Invite individuals to rate and discuss their own 'listening performances' during several recent listening experiences.
- Get individuals to rate and discuss the quality of their talk during several recent occasions when they spoke at length or took part in a group/pair interaction.

Alternatively, children can simply identify their number one choice. Urge them to justify its selection.

Another option is 'Preferences'. Get children to compare and contrast two experiences of listening or of talk, stating which they preferred. Ask them *what* they preferred about the experience (easier to answer than *why*).

> ## DIFFERENTIATION
>
> Invite adventurous thinkers, speakers or listeners to do one of the above rating activities using a criterion of their own, e.g. funniest, most boring, hardest, most surprising, most interesting, longest.

Recommendations

Ask children to give these orally, either by turning to a partner or addressing a group. Where possible they should make them to a motivating audience, for example, friends unfamiliar with the 'item' recommended, a visitor to the class or children in role (e.g. as uninformed children from another period in history!). Some ideas for recommendations are:

- The 'top three' – or one – chosen item/s from the 'rating and choosing' list above.
- A subject or topic of conversation they love talking about.
- A type of radio or TV programme, or live entertainment, they love listening to and/or watching.
- Top tips for speaking to a particular audience in a particular space and context, e.g. recounting winning a prize to the whole school in assembly.

Ensure that children explain *why* they are making their recommendations.

DIFFERENTIATION

Ask speakers who need an extra challenge to play devil's advocate sometimes, i.e. perhaps to find three 'good things' to recommend even in something they do/did *not* enjoy. Suggest to children who need support such speaking frames as 'You would really like/enjoy *x* because . . .', 'The special thing about *x* is . . .' or 'The reason I chose *x* is . . .'. Rephrase your questioning about *why* speakers are making certain recommendations if they find 'Why?' questions hard. Ask instead, '*What* do you like/find exciting, helpful, etc. about *x*?' (This directs them to list specific aspects of the recommended 'item'.) If they are recommending a programme, play or show, it may help if they describe three important parts of or events in it first.

Reviewing talk

Reviews can happen after children have given a talk or presentation, conducted an interview, issued instructions, taken part in pair or group discussion or undertaken a drama activity. Before they do the original task, ask them to remain alert throughout as to how they are tackling it, and in what order. Afterwards, ask at least some of them to outline to you and/or their peers:

- what the task was (e.g. interviewing the 'town planner' in role as characters from Mairi Hedderwick's *Katie Morag* books about the development of the jetty);
- what they did, in what sequence (e.g. decided what their ideas were about developing the jetty, planned questions to ask, role-played asking questions as *x* character, listened and responded to the answers, then decided afterwards in groups if their views had changed); and
- what features their oracy task had, using the metalanguage (specialist terminology) of oracy as much as possible (e.g. 'brainstorming', 'planning', 'questions', 'role-play', 'interview', 'point of view', 'interruption', 'agreed', 'disagreed').

In addition, especially with confident speakers and listeners, prime them to be aware, while they are speaking and listening, of:

- how they reacted to the task (e.g. immediately recalling other similar tasks, feeling unsure about some aspects, wondering where to start, coping well or otherwise with the talking and listening required);

- what they thought during the task (e.g. if they found some parts hard or easy, what they liked or disliked about the task, and how they resolved problems such as getting stuck, not hearing, not being heard or disagreeing);

- what helped them during the task (e.g. asking someone else for ideas, asking speakers to repeat or clarify what they said, recall of similar tasks); and

- their immediate feelings about the task at the end of the session (e.g. how well they think they have done, what they think they have learnt or wish they had done differently, and what they regard as their speaking and listening strengths and weaknesses).

Ask at least some children to feed back to you and/or their peers on these aspects too.

Getting used to 'observing themselves at work' in this way, on a regular basis, heightens children's powers of metacognition.

DIFFERENTIATION

Invite children who are especially alert to their thought processes to represent them diagrammatically, perhaps in emoticons (a simple facial expression symbol representing an emotion) accompanying headings describing the different parts of the task (e.g. Deciding your ideas about the jetty, Planning questions to ask, Interviewing, Looking back at your ideas in a group).

Uncertain children, particularly children with recall problems, should summarise the processes involved in the task *immediately* after they finish; you may need to give them shorter oracy tasks in the first place. Ask thinkers who struggle 'closed' questions, e.g. if they can't remember the details of the example task above, ask whether it was to persuade the 'planner' not to develop the jetty, to ask him to rebuild the jetty or to interview him about the reasons for its development; if they are unsure what they thought while interviewing, ask them whether they found it easy to remember their questions, whether they understood the answers and how well they coped with responding to these with yet more questions.

Evaluations

Four sub-categories of this approach are described below.

Giving opinions

After any of the listening experiences suggested above, ask children *either* what they think of, *or* how they would describe:

- that kind of experience (e.g. listening to audio-books generally);
- the way the speaker/s spoke (e.g. tone of voice, volume, pace, rhythm, clarity, etc.);

- the language used by the speaker/s (e.g. their vocabulary, any dialect, accent, typical phraseology, etc.);
- the most striking facts, descriptions or episodes from the experience (quote examples); or
- their own listening performance.

One approach is to ask each child for a 'snap judgement' on this, in one or two words initially (you may wish to jot their ideas down); then to discuss the 'item', e.g. a particular speaker's use of language, in more depth; and finally to invite the children to revise their initial impressions (recording any changes). Praise listeners who are able to extend their first responses.

An alternative approach is to select one appropriate aspect listed above and to ask:

- 'Do/did you like it? Why?'
- 'Do/did you find it difficult, fun, funny, interesting, surprising, scary, etc? Why?'

Also, periodically ask them about themselves as speakers or as listeners:

- What do they consider their strengths and weaknesses?
- What kinds of listening do they like and dislike?
- What kinds of talk do they like and dislike?
- What kinds of audience do they find it easier and harder to talk with or to?

Jotting down their responses – or asking them to, for example in a learning journal – provides invaluable information about children as speakers, listeners and learners; it also heightens their self-awareness (metacognition).

DIFFERENTIATION

Much of the above describes an open-ended approach, especially suited to able thinkers and speakers. In a mixed-ability setting, give uncertain children a limited choice of responses; for example, when asking them to evaluate the way a speaker spoke, invite them to choose between descriptions such as 'lively', 'varied', 'full of expression', 'unclearly', 'flatly', 'quietly', etc. Where listeners struggle to explain *why* they liked or disliked a listening experience or found it hard to understand, ask them instead to explain *what* they liked, disliked or found difficult.

Judging

After a listening experience of any kind (hearing a talk, a storytelling, an audiobook or a presentation, or watching drama, a TV programme or a video), canvass children's judgements on one or two of the following. Ask them whether:

- they would want to save and keep the experience in a small imaginary 'listening suitcase' or not;
- they liked or disliked it (and how much, e.g. on a scale of 1 to 5);

- they found it boring or entertaining/interesting (and how much, e.g. on a scale of 1 to 5);
- it held any surprises;
- it made them want to hear more of the same or similar;
- they found it hard or easy to follow; and/or
- they were pleased with their own 'listening performance'.

Ask children for a show of hands for and against the listening experience, or undertake a 'secret ballot' on pieces of paper. Welcome diverse responses: celebrate non-conformity. Over a period of time, you may wish to build up a star rating system for listening experiences the class or group has enjoyed.

DIFFERENTIATION

Introduce children alert to the subtleties of vocabulary to words of different 'intensities', matched, say, to the numbers 1 to 5 in a scale; for instance, if asking them to judge the interest of a listening experience, invite them to choose from a spectrum of terms from 'dull' to 'factual', to 'interesting', to 'fact-packed' and 'fascinating'.

Critical talk friends

It may be that your children are already in 'talk partnerships', i.e. pairings for the pooling and discussion of ideas in one or more areas of the curriculum. However, beware: children may be well-matched for some subjects or activities and not for others. It often works to partner twos who would not choose each other, avoiding both close friendships and 'difficult' combinations!

Ask suitable talk pairs to sit together for any task where you expect a 'spoken product', whether shared between them or from each as an individual, for example, a theory, a plan, an account of an activity undertaken, a presentation, a story-telling or a response to a listening experience such as a TV programme. Nominate one in each pair as A, the other as B. Invite A to express and develop his/her ideas first, and B to comment on them; after an appropriate time, or at a signal from you, B can express his/her ideas and A can comment. (If you are happy for pairs to develop a shared spoken outcome, now ask them to negotiate until they have reached agreement on its form: setting a time limit helps.) Set criteria for partners to use when commenting on each other's ideas, for instance:

- If individuals are preparing what to say about a TV programme they have just watched, you might pre-set as indicators of success (a) their mentioning three facts, descriptions or episodes from the programme, and (b) their stating one thing they liked or disliked about each. Pairs can judge if partners have met these criteria.
- If pairs are deciding on a joint theory about why one object sank in water while another floated, you might give as the criteria for an effective theory (a) their describing at least one feature of water, (b) their describing at least one

feature of each object, and (c) their inclusion of at least one idea from each child. Partners can again self-judge against these criteria.

Whether children are commenting on each other's ideas or actually pooling them, praise those who use your criteria, advise each other sensitively, listen to their partners and adjust their thinking accordingly.

Finally, ensure that plenty of individuals or pairs have time to share their spoken 'product' aloud with the wider group or class.

DIFFERENTIATION

Set different 'levels' of criteria for different abilities of children, and/or more for the able, fewer for the less confident.

Other kinds of collaboration

Often pairs or groups work together through talk and other 'media', for example in experiments, investigations, artwork, constructions, research, surveys, ICT projects or rehearsed pieces of drama. Before they begin, set certain criteria for 'talk success'. Ideally, these should be brainstormed, discussed and negotiated with the children. Some of these criteria might be:

- a method agreed and used for taking turns, or everyone taking part, in the doing and/or speaking;
- everyone's part to be clearly visible in the finished product (e.g. by annotation with the children's initials);
- the 'right kind of talk' to be used, e.g. suggesting and planning, or theorising and commenting, or describing and informing; and
- if roles are adopted (e.g. chairperson, scribe, doer/maker, interviewer, spokesperson), children to stick to these roles and to use the kind of talk associated with them.

Afterwards, invite at least some children to evaluate orally how well their groups/pairs did according to the criteria agreed.

If some kind of drama is the final outcome, you may wish to set further criteria for the success of the finished piece against which the class or group can judge it, for instance whether it illustrates the subject or content asked for, clear voice projection, expressiveness of voice and gestures, memorable word choices, use of the whole space provided, etc.

DIFFERENTIATION

Extend the skills of the critically mature and orally able by designating them as 'talk monitors' in group work. Put them in charge of:

- reminding children of the 'right kind of talk' (see above), modelling examples and suggesting 'sentence frames' if necessary (e.g. 'What about if we . . .?' for tasks involving suggesting and planning);

- doing the same for children with specific roles within the group (e.g. reminding the scribe to say 'What shall I write now?', or 'How shall I put that down?'); and

- recording or remembering particularly effective examples of talk, agreement, constructive criticism, etc.

Even the least confident 'self-critics' can give a 'thumbs-up' (or down) in evaluation of such collaborative talk – ideally against several criteria, not just the talk task as a whole. For the benefit of the less self-aware, from time to time video such sessions, or specific groups or pairs working within such sessions. Play the film back and invite evaluations against criteria such as those suggested above, thus sharpening their self-critical faculties.

Affective thinking and emotional literacy

Tracking thoughts and feelings . . .

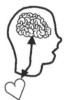

In a range of learning contexts, draw children's attention to the wide variety of human emotions: anger, fear, happiness, sadness, anxiety, disgust, surprise, like, dislike. . . . Consider together the differences in people's body language and behaviour when experiencing each of these emotions, and the kinds of situations that provoke them. (Avoid labelling some emotions as 'good' and others as 'bad'. Stress that all feelings are valid in certain contexts; promote the importance of recognising and managing them well.) You may find it useful collaboratively to devise an emoticon (a simple facial expression symbol representing an emotion) for each feeling discussed; display them somewhere, for instance on a poster, for classroom use in a wide range of learning contexts. The following sub-categories of approach allow you to build on such work.

. . . through listening to fiction or recount

Undertake this activity when children have:

- watched and listened to a DVD, video or TV story or real-life recount (told or enacted);

- seen a group, class or school performance of fictional or actual events; or

- listened to a story, true or imagined.

Suitable accounts are those in which the feelings of one or more characters change, either explicitly or by implication. Invite children to record such fluctuations, using a set of class emoticons or some of their own devising. They can draw or stick these symbols in a sequence on a blank piece of paper, shadowing, as it were, the 'emotional shape' of the account.

After any such listening activity, encourage children to share and compare similar experiences and emotions they have known in their own lives.

. . . through drama about problems and relationships

We are often aware of emotional and relationship issues that preoccupy children. Many need sensitive handling, but common themes include:

- the absence of one or more family members;
- bereavement and loss;
- teasing and bullying;
- fickle friendships;
- envy and copying (peer pressure);
- feeling left out or inferior;
- new siblings (or adults) in the home; and
- shyness and uncertainty.

These powerful subjects are often best tackled through the objectivity of drama. Improvisation and role-play can provide a safety net for difficult feelings, and can even help develop children's thought in constructive ways by throwing up coping strategies and solutions. (Consult parents fully in relation to some topics before beginning.)

Pick one or more of the themes above, as appropriate to children's needs. *Without* drawing attention to any relevant recent experiences, ask children, in small groups with trusted peers, to develop scenarios based on their allocated theme. Get them to 'freeze-frame' mid-dialogue or -action, and ask all – including the actors – to suggest out loud what the 'characters' might be thinking or feeling. Alternatively, if the children already have a 'class bank' of emoticons (see page 27), give spectators a selection, printed on cards or drawn on small whiteboards, and invite them to raise those they think reflect the participants' feelings most accurately. Another option is to issue each spectator with a small whiteboard with a think bubble drawn on it. At key moments in the drama, with the actors 'freeze-framed', invite the 'audience' to write in their bubbles what they guess one character is thinking or feeling. Again, discuss their ideas carefully. Do the actors agree? This work can be completed by brainstorming a list of useful coping strategies and recording them in some form, e.g. a poster for the wall, pamphlets for 'friendship monitors' in the playground, or advice stuck in home-school diaries.

> ## DIFFERENTIATION
>
> Never insist all children participate; consult with them, and with their parents well in advance if you are in any doubt whether to involve them. (Even observing such activities silently may help develop the thinking of children with relevant problems.) Challenge more capable speakers to invent their own scenarios. Give less confident actors a more closed brief, for example, if asking them to enact a teasing scene give them specific parts, such as a girl on the climbing frame and two older boys from another class, and perhaps suggest the first two lines of dialogue. It may also inspire children if you show a suitable film clip or read a relevant text before beginning.

Risk-taking

Openly discuss, and value with speakers and listeners, their ability and willingness to take risks; stress that risk-taking, i.e. trying unfamiliar things, is the only way learners learn. Challenge children sometimes to be 'brave enough' to make a choice or take a risk they would prefer not to. Some examples of speaking and listening that encourage risk-taking are:

- any listening experience with no preamble from the teacher explaining what it will be!
- working on an improvisation or role-play with a limited brief, e.g. simply a theme, as in the previous activity;
- a 'difficult listen' that requires intelligent guesses, e.g. about word meanings, or 'off-stage' events;
- a first-time speaking part in a performance;
- new demands while speaking or reading, e.g. to use new, specialist vocabulary, or to use expression;
- working with an unfamiliar or unchosen partner or group; and
- taking on a new speaking role during group discussion and collaborative work, e.g. chairperson or reporter to the class.

Ideas from earlier sections

Many suggestions from earlier sections can contribute to affective thinking and emotional literacy. The following sub-sections recap on these.

Problem-solving

Allowing children to make at least some choices in their speaking and/or listening ('Making choices', page 11) empowers them, giving them a sense of ownership of their learning activity. It often boosts their motivation, not to mention their self-esteem.

Under 'Exploring dilemmas' (page 15), it is suggested that children should make 'real-life transference': give them the chance to share analogous experiences of their own, and to consider what they did, or would do, in similar situations.

Creative thinking

Asking children 'How many ways can you describe . . .?' (page 17) or 'How many words would fit?' in 'Memory jogger' (page 18) encourages them to be flexible and wide-ranging in their thinking – a quality some term 'fluency'.

'Same words, different meaning' (page 19) throws the spotlight on the wide range of human emotions and the body language that we use to express them.

Critical thinking

The 'Recommendations' approach (pages 21–2) asks children to champion their own listening preferences, no matter how at variance with their peers'; it exposes them to the varied tastes of others, and encourages them to not to be frightened of being different.

The opinion-giving and judging activities under 'Evaluations' (page 23) also encourage differing viewpoints, plus tolerance of those of others.

If a group or pair decision is required for any of the 'Rating and choosing' activities described on pages 20–1, this stimulates the development of children's interpersonal skills: their abilities to listen to and appreciate others' ideas, lead or include other group members, negotiate and, where necessary, compromise. The same is true of 'Critical talk friends' (page 25) and 'Other kinds of collaboration' (page 26) – in fact, any other speaking and listening activities in which several children are required to produce a joint or single outcome.

Slotting approaches together

Many of the approaches described in 'Problem-solving', 'Creative thinking' and 'Critical thinking' – and in this section too – can be 'slotted together' to create an extended block of work if desired. Each phase should take children's thinking about their speaking and/or listening to a new level. This in-depth approach will help them develop 'learning stamina', one facet of affective thinking.

Questioning skills

With children, emphasise the importance of questioning. Since real engagement in learning *requires* a spirit of enquiry, stress that questioning should be the mode of much pupil talk, not just of teacher talk. Many KS1 classrooms prominently display the so-called 'question words' so that children can use them as prompts to aid question formulation. Getting them to practise devising interesting and appropriate questions beginning 'Who?', 'What?', 'When?', 'Where?', 'Why?' and 'How?'

steers children away from too often starting questions with words like 'Do/Does?', or 'Is/Are?', which tend to 'narrow down' information given in reply to 'Yes' or 'No'!

Formats and games

The following sub-categories of formats and games emphasise oral questioning skills, inviting children to practise using searching question words.

Interviews across the curriculum

Ask children to:

- watch/listen to interviews, for example, on TV or during role-play (help them to notice the 'best'/most interesting questions, transcribe them and perhaps categorise them, e.g. according to how they are worded or the sub-topics covered);
- interview tour guides, school visitors, subject experts and speakers;
- question people in the course of surveys;
- video conference, e.g. with subject experts; or
- interrogate adults or peers in role, e.g. through hotseating, role-playing TV broadcasts or questioning puppets or soft toys (for example in circle time).

Teacher statements

From time to time, use a single introductory statement to begin a new subject topic or to mark a new phase of activity within a unit of work, for example, 'There are four seasons in the year', or 'Taking-away in maths is hard'. Make it orally, and/or write and display it clearly somewhere, e.g. on a board. Invite children's comments or questions in response, remaining silent except to act as 'chairperson', encouraging contributors and conducting the discussion as it continues. (If this is a new format, it may take children a while, and lots of encouragement, to get going!) Recording what they say can be fascinating and informative, revealing high-level thinking and learning and providing detail that may aid the planning of future teaching as well as assessment. Don't be fooled: many remarks will probably be questions in disguise: 'I thought there were only two seasons in some countries' would be a welcome and knowledgeable challenge to the above pronouncement on seasons, while 'I can't do taking-away at all' in response to the teacher's subtraction comment above should be recognised as another kind of question – an honest request for help!

Barrier games

The teacher or a child conceals a picture or object. One or more others should attempt to guess what it is, or to draw it, through dialogue and close questioning.

Who/what am I?

Sticker the foreheads of one or more children with a label stating who or what they are. They should try to guess their 'identities' by questioning others. (Alternatively, children can be asked to write labels for each other.) If you like, labels can be confined to people, animals or things connected with a topic being studied.

Telephone mystery

Privately brief a child to behave in role as if they have just experienced a funny or disastrous situation of your choosing, e.g. bumping into their reflection in a mirror. Explain that they must not use body language, gestures or certain key words, e.g. 'mirror', 'reflection', or of course explain their scenario directly. Another child must question them in a 'telephone conversation', ideally aided by a real or toy telephone, until they establish what has happened.

DIFFERENTIATION

During the pair games above, encourage children watching to propose appropriate questions for the players to ask. Record, display and celebrate especially good ones, taking class votes on them if desired. Debate which kinds of question are hardest to form, and why. ('Why?' and 'How?' questions are especially challenging to formulate; they also invite a wider range of answers, which can be longer and more interesting.) Challenge confident questioners to formulate 'How?', 'What/Which?' and 'Why?' questions. They can also try to supplement 'How?' questions with an adjective or adverb – 'How much?', 'How big?', 'How quickly?' – and 'What?/Which?' questions with a noun or noun phrase – 'What kind of . . .?', 'Which colour?' (Suggest appropriate supplementary words if they are struggling.) Encourage them to probe or challenge the replies they get, e.g. 'What do you mean by . . .?', 'How do you know . . .?' If they have been spectating at an interview, invite able thinkers, listeners and questioners to categorise the questions they have heard into groupings of their own devising.

Give unconfident questioners the prompts 'When?', 'Where?' and 'Who?' Suggest to struggling questioners one or two other key words beside the best 'question word', for example, to encourage a child to ask where the best place is to plant some seeds, suggest 'Where?', 'best' and 'plant'.

Unfinished business

At the end of a unit of work or subject topic, ask children to volunteer questions they would still like answered. Useful sentence frames are: 'I would still like to know what/where/when/how/who/why/if/whether . . .', and 'Next time we study/do *x*, I wish I could/would like to/would rather . . .' Children's responses should inform both your future planning and your assessment of their learning; as suggested earlier, their 'answers' will actually be questions in disguise!

DIFFERENTIATION

Challenge more able speakers to devise their own questions without suggesting 'sentence frames' they might use.

PLAN-DO-REVIEW FORMATS: A CASE STUDY

The following two examples of Speaking and Listening activity were incorporated in a unit of work at Year 1 around *The Little Red Hen*, a traditional story with predictable and repetitive patterns, including those of language, available in many published versions. The work developed problem-solving, creative and critical thinking, emotional literacy and questioning skills. Lessons followed the sequence of 'plan-do-review', similar to that promoted by Belle Wallace in her TASC problem-solving wheel (see Introduction, page 4). The activities aimed to develop four strands of oracy: group discussion, drama, 'long-turn' speaking and 'long-turn' listening.

Group discussion and role-play: sharing the red hen's chores

Different children were made aware of the different learning outcomes I expected from them, as described here.

Learning objectives (for the group discussion described below): All children to contribute at least one idea within a group (problem-solving), and to take turns at speaking; some to suggest *various* ways of whole-group participation during this discussion, and of undertaking the role-play task to follow (creative thinking); some to administer turn-taking sensitively (emotional literacy); and a few to propose logistical reasons for their idea/s working in practice (problem-solving).

Learning objectives (for the role-play described below): All children to empathise with a well-known character through improvisation and role-play (emotional literacy); some to deal maturely with conflict during role-play (problem-solving and emotional literacy); and a few to perceive and express the relevance of role-play to their own experiences (emotional literacy and critical thinking).

The role-play also facilitated learning objectives on the writing of information texts (including captions), lists, instructions and signs.

The first lesson
Through discussion of housework in their own homes, reading the text and word and sentence study, especially of the tale's patterned events and language, the children already knew the story and its theme of the struggle with housework, and could recite large parts by heart. I appeared now in role as the little red hen (wearing an apron, with a red paper 'comb' attached to a hairband on my head and a couple of feathers pinned to my 'tail'!). Pointing to the classroom's kitchen corner, I demanded tearfully that since the animals in the story had failed to help 'me' with the bread-making, from now on they must help with other chores.

I divided the children into fours/fives, ability-matched according to their problem-solving skills and with at least one 'emotionally mature' child in each group. I then supplied each group with rough paper, pencils and crayons; in addition they had a page of pictorial symbols, captioned, representing five different household chores: oven cleaning, floor sweeping, dusting, table laying and dishwashing. I explained that the children must decide in their separate groups how five kinds of farm animal – pigs, ducks, cows, horses and sheep – could do these tasks every day over a week (while I, the red hen, stuck to cooking!). I also gave each group a page illustrated with the five animals above, as reminders of the 'characters' to do the chores.

First, I invited groups to establish how we could ensure that everyone, on each table, had a say in any decisions. I stressed that this thinking was already work, the work of problem-solving (although many did not comprehend this term, I interpreted it as the task of 'sorting out difficult jobs': what was difficult about it, I expanded, was that unless a method was found, children might all talk at once, or some feel left out). They conferred for a few moments; I circulated, noting who expressed sensible, varied or original ideas. We pooled the children's thoughts. (Those with several were exhibiting not just problem-solving but creative thinking skills.) The ideas included putting hands up; taking it in turns to speak clockwise, anti-clockwise or alphabetically round the table; passing an object round, and only speaking when they held it; and a variety of other signals, e.g. waving a flag! I drew symbols on the board to represent each suggestion, and invited comments on disadvantages the children perceived with any of the suggestions (critical thinking). Alphabetical order, for instance, was stated to be unfair; one child noted that it would 'take too much time' to make flags! I pointed out, since no one else had, that using the signal of a raised hand might exclude some children from the process. The class then voted on their preferred method (more critical thinking), which turned out to be passing an object around the group, thus ensuring and controlling each child's contribution.

I gave an 'emotionally mature' member of each group a coloured plastic cube as the object to be passed round, and put them in charge of monitoring fair play with it. Next I issued less confident problem-solving groups with scissors, glue and a five-day timetable labelled Monday–Friday, whose grid of squares was big enough to take the cut-up pictures of chores and animals I had supplied – either all, or just some, for each day. (Particularly diffident children were given just one day in the week to think about.) I withheld these resources from the most adventurous problem-solvers, instead giving them free rein on the allocation and organisation of the housework, challenging them to think of *several* ways of doing it, not just one (creative thinking); meanwhile, as discussion got under way, I suggested to any 'middle' groups – whom I had not issued with the grid of days either – that they might like to devise some kind of daily timetable (pointing out our own lesson timetable on the classroom wall as an example).

During fifteen minutes of circulating to monitor this discussion activity, I pressed the unconfident to see that there was more than one way of filling in their timetables (creative thinking); supported 'middling' groups in how to draw up a usable timetable format in the first place (problem-solving); and challenged the most adventurous not only to think of several ideas, but to devise ones that might surprise others, then to rank them from the most popular to the least favoured amongst their group (critical thinking). As for the 'chairs', I quietly encouraged them to extend their role by making tactful, helpful remarks, for example urging a group member to do more than repeat a fellow member's idea; ensuring that their whole group took turns with any physical task; or encouraging a child who was reluctant to participate (emotional literacy).

At the end of this process, several groups had spokespeople confident enough to show and/or explain their ideas to the class (I had not insisted on their recording them); I summarised and/or showed other groups' suggestions. I especially noted those children who had thought through how they, in role as 'animals', could 'help the hen' in the kitchen area within the practicalities of a bustling classroom week (able problem-solvers indeed!). Comments and questions from the class about each group's work were encouraged (critical thinking). I highlighted and praised examples of problem-solving and creative thinking, trying to find instances from each group, and repeatedly using these novel terms!

The next five lessons

On the next Monday, I arrived with a list of every group's housework solutions (some, if unrecorded, I had noted down). I had cleared a large display area and headed it 'Message Board'. First of all, we briefly recapped and discussed as a class the merits of each idea on the list, then the class voted on their preferred plan of action (critical thinking, ensuring affective connection with the work: the class felt they had 'ownership' of the selected idea). The 'winning' solution timetabled the chores for every day: dishwashing and oven cleaning, sensibly, were to happen before dusting and floor sweeping, which, again sensibly, would be done before table laying; furthermore, a different kind of animal was responsible for each job – *and* an effort had been made by the 'winning' problem-solving group to suit the animal to the chore, e.g., ducks would clean the oven because they were shorter, and would not need to bend!

Once more in role as the harassed red hen, I stickered each child's chest with a label on which I had printed a sketch of a pig, sheep, horse, duck or cow. I explained to the class that we would follow the particular rota voted for. (A daily 'housework group' was to consist of one child in role as each of the five animals, plus the odd 'extra'. Children were grouped according to their confidence at role-play, and compatible personalities.) I addressed each child as 'their' animal, e.g. 'Mr Pig', whilst they were in role.

On each day that week, one group of children performed 'their' five household chores in role in the kitchen area for a maximum of ten minutes while the rest of the class watched. They then wrote a message on a Post-it® and stuck it on my 'Message Board', telling me (the hen) that they had done their chore (some drew, some used emergent writing and/or basic phonics with gaps for unknown sounds). Throughout I urged them to remember how 'their' particular animal might behave – willingly or reluctantly, efficiently or badly, and with appropriate sound effects and movements. They also had to show the audience how they were 'suited' to the task they had been given (e.g. a child might decide that when dishwashing as a sheep, they could rub the dishes with their wool!). All considerations were intended to develop empathy with 'their' characters. During the role-play, to encourage 'emotional maturity', I questioned some about how to resolve conflict as it arose, e.g. near-collisions in the kitchen area and disputes, for instance over sequencing of tasks. (One child suggested speaking politely to others, another stopping the whole group to confer on how to resolve the difficulty. I especially encouraged polite questioning as a way out of difficulties.) I asked the audience about these scenarios' relevance to their home life: several were able to perceive links, for example, complaints about family members 'getting under parents' feet', or some people's avoidance of the chores!

After five days, children's strategies for working together had improved dramatically, as had their confidence as role-players (diffident groups role-played later in the week, so that they had already observed more able children's acting); and the whole class had become keen to draw unusual parallels with, and to retell interesting anecdotes from, their home life!

The final lesson

A parent helper had taken digital photos of some role-play and class discussion as the week progressed. I now showed these to the children, explaining that they were to form a display on a corridor board. I invited the class to interview each group of role-players in turn, devising questions beginning 'Who?', 'How did you?', 'What did you?' or 'Why did you?' (i.e. based on the question words on the wall beside me). These questions, I explained, must establish what had gone well and what could have worked better about the timetabling activity, the group work and the role-play, thus developing questioning skills and critical thinking. (I prompted diffident questioners with several words and phrases to help them frame their questions, e.g., 'How did you?', 'well' and 'as a group'.)

Interviewing over, I then encouraged the children – back in their 'home' groups of the first lesson, and working in pairs/threes – to co-write either wording for captions for the photos (in the case of emergent writers), or a piece of information text to describe the whole housework scenario to others (in the case of writers with phonics whose metacognitive skills, i.e. thinking about their learning, was evolving). The most advanced thinkers were asked to write a list of instructions or a moral, whether about working as a group, or helping others with housework at home (I had asked them to read morals, or stories with morals, with their families for homework beforehand).

Long-turn speaking and long-turn listening: storytelling new versions of *The Little Red Hen*

Learning objectives (for the long-turn speaking described below): All children to order events in a story appropriately and logically when retelling them (problem-solving); some to make imaginative links between the events (creative thinking); and a few to design and/or use a *range* of 'speaking frames', and patterned story language, when telling their stories (creative thinking).

Learning objectives (for the long-turn listening described below): All children to listen to the stories being told, showing sustained concentration through their identification of the order of events and emotions of characters (problem-solving and emotional literacy); some to express a view about how the stories were told (critical thinking); and a few to justify these views by quoting details or providing evidence (critical thinking).

The first lesson
As soon as possible after the lesson sequence above, and following a reread of the original *Little Red Hen* story, I issued:

- pairs of diffident speakers with a set of copies of four digital photos, taken by the parent helper, of their animal role-play, jumbled up;

- pairs of more confident thinkers and speakers with a set of six pictures, which I had sketched and photocopied. Three were of a pig, duck, sheep, horse and cow: in one, all looking grumpy; in another, doing household chores, clearly getting under each others' feet; and in another, all looking happy. Three more were of the little red hen – in one, doing several chores herself and looking distraught; in another, asleep in bed, looking contented; and in a third, in the doorway of the kitchen, looking surprised;

- individual, more able thinkers and speakers with this same set of six pictures plus a list of 'story sentences' about *another* set of animals. These included such sentences as 'A snail, owl and frog were very lazy', 'They never helped the mouse, who was always busy', 'She worked and she worked and she worked – until one day she stopped', 'That day the others saw how tired she was', etc.

The children's first job was to order their pictures into a sequence of their choice that they could 'talk through' as the outline plan for a new story (problem-solving and creative thinking). I stressed that there was no 'right' order: I wanted workable, and imaginative, solutions. This – as with the previous tasks – necessitated emotional literacy: collaboration, turn-taking, fair apportionment of effort, etc. (For the lower-ability groups, I described the behaviours I expected to see as evidence of these before they began, e.g. children looking at each other, sharing resources out and talking one at a time.) The task, furthermore, demanded logic: planners had to be able to justify their sequences to a third party (me, as I circulated, listening and questioning), and to describe any intended links between events *not* represented in the pictures themselves. I urged partners to question each other closely too, testing their own logic, for example, 'But what happens then?', or 'Why is the hen in bed?' (questioning skills).

The most advanced thinkers had another task to do: underlining and then rewriting any words and phrases, from their list of sentences, they felt could be re-used in the oral telling of their newly sequenced stories about the farm animals, in other words identifying 'speaking frames', such as 'A —, —, —, — and — were very lazy.' They then had to write beside these any other forms of words that could be used instead, e.g., 'There was once a —, —, —, — and a —' would be an alternative to the above example. Finally, all children Blu-tacked their pictures, in their chosen order, on to a long piece of card, to act as a storyboard during the actual storytelling.

The second lesson

While the pairs, seated, rehearsed their storytelling quietly together, the most capable individuals were asked to cut out and stick on, or rewrite under their storyboards, their final choice of 'speaking frames', many of which were noted during the previous lesson, with which to narrate each sequenced picture (problem-solving). I urged them to 'pattern' their language as much as possible, i.e. to use words and phrases they could repeat, such as 'The — cried and cried then cried some more, because she was so tired' (creative thinking). These most able children were then withdrawn with an assistant to finish this task.

Meanwhile the rest of the children, in their pairs, began telling their stories to the class: one held up their board while their partner used it as a prompt to recount events in story language. The most undeveloped analysts and listeners in the audience had been issued with pages bearing identical pictures of the five 'unhelpful' animals and the overworked hen as contained in the storyboards; more capable listeners were given sketches of numerous emoticons, also on a single page, representing three emotions – happiness, grumpiness and surprise. While they listened to at least one story, they were asked to number these pictures to represent the sequence in which the animals were involved in the story or emotions were expressed. (Afterwards, I asked some listeners to show and explain their records of this 'patterning': many had done well.)

The withdrawn group returned for part of the lesson. They joined the listeners at first, and while the rest continued with their numbering task during some tales, they were asked to listen for words and phrases that they especially liked. After listening, they were invited to recall some. The most articulate were encouraged to say *why* they liked them; where they struggled, I reworded my enquiry as '*What* did you like about the word/phrase . . .?', which children found easier to answer – especially when I invited them to begin, 'I liked the way it . . .' (critical thinking).

The third and fourth lessons

Children who had not yet storytold did so in these final lessons. To promote sustained attentive listening from the audience, I asked groups of six confident actors from the audience to try to enact the story being told, while it was told, in mimed role-play. Now, during the feedback I invited after each tale, many more children beside the most confident critics could recall words, phrases and patterned language that they had particularly noted and enjoyed, and quite a few could state *what* they had enjoyed about them (critical thinking). I encouraged able questioners to take over from me and quiz the storytellers, e.g. 'Why did you choose the word — ?', etc., and the audience, e.g. 'What did you like about the part when — ?' (questioning skills). To finish, we took a vote on which stories the children considered the most imaginative, and the best told (yet more critical thinking).

Reading

Many approaches described in this chapter are equally suited to shared, guided and group reading, or adapt easily to fit these contexts. A good number can also provide a focus during children's independent reading time, or they can be undertaken (or part-undertaken) at home. Where specific texts are mentioned, they are in print at the time of writing, or seen as 'classic texts', present in many school collections. However, they are given only as examples, and many others are equally appropriate.

Problem-solving

The analytical aspect of reading – thinking about the way texts work – is often recognised as critical thinking, and 'solving the "problem" of' texts. But reading involves problem-solving in other ways. First, readers must learn to 'decode' print, i.e. to solve its 'code of marks'; second, texts present deeper puzzles and dilemmas – some with definite 'answers', some without – as described below.

Finding shapes, finding patterns

Texts have what could be called 'shapes' and 'patterns'. The notion of 'shape' describes the distinctive way in which a text is organised and sequenced, e.g. with all its events building up to a climax, or with an ending that mirrors the beginning in some way. The notion of 'pattern' describes any form of repetition, for example, characteristics of the layout that are the same on each page; a consistent rhyme scheme; a repeated phrase, idea or image; or events that recur in a story. (Of course, writers also 'break' patterns for effect.) The following sub-categories of activity heighten children's awareness of such features. Undertake them only when children are familiar with your chosen text.

Mapping and tracking

In many stories and some poems, the main characters travel through various settings, for example in numerous traditional tales, Pat Hutchins' *Rosie's Walk* or Helen Nicoll's *Mog in the Fog*. Ask children to draw a map showing the character's journey. They should draw each setting visited, in the right sequence, linked together by a road or path (with the character/s travelling along the route, if desired). If each setting occurs only once in the original text, the route they draw should look fairly linear; if some are revisited, it may zigzag, or indeed take a circular shape if the initial setting recurs at the end of the story. In cross-curricular texts, journeys also occur. After studying accounts of the Christmas story, ask children to map the travels of the Holy Family, the shepherds and the wise men: this should result in pictures along three routes converging on the nativity scene in Bethlehem. On the other hand, reading accounts of a river's journey to the sea, e.g. Meredith Hooper's *River Story*, should suggest a linear map in which the 'route' is the river itself, widening as it passes through different settings.

DIFFERENTIATION

Children unfamiliar with such activities may benefit from hearing the text with their eyes closed, trying to visualise the various places mentioned. Do not remind confident 'trackers' of all the settings in the original text; however, give unconfident 'trackers', or those with recall problems, a list or pictorial symbols for all these in random order. Challenge the children to sequence them appropriately in their maps.

Other stories and poems revolve around meetings between various characters at different points. For instance, in Claudia Fries's *A Pig Is Moving In!*, first the fox meets the pig, then he talks to the hen, then the hen meets the pig, then the hen talks to the hare, and so on. Children can record these meetings in a series of pictures joined by a path. They can depict the characters who 'move on' to meet others as walking along this 'path'.

DIFFERENTIATION

Do not remind confident 'trackers' of all the meetings in the original text; however, give unconfident 'trackers', or those with recall problems, a list or pictorial symbols representing all the meetings, in random order. Challenge the children to sequence them appropriately in their maps.

In some stories, it is the appearance, behaviour or mood of a character that changes. For example, Michael Morpurgo's *Rainbow Bear* changes from a free and happy snow-white bear at the beginning, to a miserable caged 'rainbow bear' in the middle, and back to his old self at the end. From a suitable text you have been studying, ask children to draw a picture of the character who changes, fairly small, without his or her arms or facial features. Photocopy these drawings several times for each child. Give them the photocopies, and ask them to draw in different facial expressions, with the arms in different expressive positions, on each copy to show the change in the character in its various phases. They should then number these in sequence on the reverse. You can now make flick books (with the first picture at the back, the last at the front); these will graphically 'track' the changes in a character.

Do not remind confident children of the main changes in the text; however, give less confident children a series of pictorial symbols representing all these, out of order; ask them to sequence them, following the 'shape' of the text.

Other stories have a strong causal element, i.e. one event or action leads directly to another. For example, in Ruth Brown's *The Big Sneeze*, the farmer's sneezing sets off animal noise and flap, which gradually 'ripples out' to cause ever greater chaos in the barn. Non-fiction texts describing processes, such as how a bee makes honey, or a metamorphosis from caterpillar to butterfly, also imply cause and effect. Martin Jenkins's *The Emperor's Egg* illustrates how a father penguin's dedicated egg-sitting leads to its hatching, and the mother's later arrival to his release from duty. Having read an appropriate text, ask children to draw pictures showing the events, and arrows linking them to their results.

DIFFERENTIATION

In the case of a text where only some events cause others, leave able children to remember those which are connected for themselves; however, remind children with poor recall of several *un*connected events from the original account as well – for instance, in Jez Alborough's *Duck in the Truck*, the efforts of the frog, sheep and other animals as well as those of the goat (who is the only one to help the truck get unstuck). Ask them to select only the events that 'lead to each other' for their causal maps or diagrams.

Of course, you will need to model how to do any of these mapping and tracking activities before children attempt them.

Comparing

Comparison stimulates children to see 'patterns' in the same text, or across several. It should be encouraged where there are more similarities to note than differences.

- The obvious case is word study: words in a text often have a common rhyme, sound or spelling pattern. However, you may pick out words with other common features and ask children to spot them too – the same number of syllables, for instance, or the fact that they are all connectives, proper names or adjectives. Ask them to find more examples in the studied text or other texts. The children can record their observations in some way, e.g. rewriting the words on a poster and captioning them with an explanation of the common feature.

- Children can also search for similarities in sentences, e.g. the fact that they all contain connectives, lists, speech, descriptions or a particular punctuation mark.

- Likewise similar layouts, characters, settings, dialogue or events can reoccur in texts. Again, ask the children what texts have in common – usually several features. For example, in Katharine Holabird's *Angelina and Alice* the two friends share several personality traits; in Karen Wallace's *Mothers Are Everywhere* the various common instincts and behaviours of human and animal mothers are described side by side throughout the text. Alternatively, you can ask children to compare similar aspects, for example events, in several texts. Ask them to tell you what is the same about Jill Murphy's *Peace at Last* and Mick Inkpen's *Lullabyhullaballoo!* (a single character tries to sleep and is disturbed by a series of noises); or Korky Paul's *Winnie the Witch Flies Again!* and Quentin Blake's *Mrs Armitage – Queen of the Road* (both 'heroines' suffer numerous accidents with their means of transport). Invite children to record the separate examples, e.g. in their own pictures, signposting similarities with labels. Comparison also heightens children's awareness of the layout features of non-fiction. Ask them to study books from the same non-fiction series that have a distinctive 'series style', and invite them to tell you what is the same about the way the pictures, captions, headings and main text are arranged on each page or double-page spread.

DIFFERENTIATION

For any of the above activities, encourage confident children to think independently; put unsure children in pairs or groups with trusted peers, or give them fewer features at a time for comparison.

Contrasting

Looking for contrasts stimulates children to see 'absence of pattern' within texts, or across several; it should be encouraged when there are more dissimilarities to note than similarities.

- Invite children to study words within texts that are very different, and to explain to you how and why. The obvious example is opposites (antonyms); others are contractions as opposed to the expanded, standard English equivalents (e.g. 'don't' and 'do not'); proper as opposed to common nouns; and words printed in roman, as opposed to words in bold (e.g. as headings) or italics (e.g. to convey emphasis or loudness). Invite them to 'collect' as many as possible 'contrasting words' in one or several suitable texts, and to do a presentation or poster display about them.

- Children can also study sentences that contrast. Show them instances of statements, exclamations and questions; sentences with connectives and without; or sentences in the past and present tenses. Ask them to identify how and why they differ, and to find other examples in one or several texts.

- Also draw attention to very different layouts, characters or settings within or across texts. For example, ask children to find the contrasts in illustrative style (from colour to sketchy black-and-white) within John Burningham's *Granpa*. After reading Alexis Deacon's *Slow Loris*, ask children to describe the differences in the sloth's behaviour and appearance in daytime and at night; or, having read Andrew Matthews's *Bob Robber and Dancing Jane*, to list the differences between the two characters. In any book from Jeanne Willis's *Dr Xargle* series, ask children to find as many differences as they can between the alien teacher's view of the human world and reality. Looking 'across texts', ask children to describe in precisely what ways two poems contrast in form (e.g. rhyming couplets, compared to an unrhyming 'block' of lines). Alternatively, from separate texts, invite them to 'spot the differences' in a pair of very unlike princesses, giants, pirates or cats; or two school settings, streets, far-off planets or islands. Ask them to draw two pictures, side by side, or put the texts into a display, captioning the differences.

DIFFERENTIATION

For any of these activities, encourage confident children to think independently; put unsure children in pairs or groups with trusted peers, or give them fewer features to contrast at once.

Comparing and contrasting

- From a text, show children words in which only one letter or the ending varies; the spelling differs although they share a rhyme; or which are repeated in a different size or font. Ask what is the same *and* what is different about them. If there are more examples in the text, invite children to find them. They can record this 'collection' in some way, e.g. rewriting one word and all the other versions, to the same scale, on different colours of card. These can be stuck as 'liftable flaps', one on top of the other, in an interactive, labelled display or into books.

- In a text, pick out sentences in which only one word or phrase varies, or only the font, layout or punctuation. Again, ask the children what is the same and what is different about them. They may be able to find more variants. As above, these might form an interactive display with 'liftable flaps' revealing the sentences in all their different versions.

- If they have been studying a story in which some characters are more important to the tale than others, ask children to sketch them on to an outline of a tree, placing those they consider 'major' characters near the top, and others lower down, in order of significance (or they may drag symbols for the characters on to a tree outline on an interactive whiteboard). For example, in Fiona French's *Anancy and Mr Dry-Bone*, they can decide whether Anancy deserves a higher place on the diagram than Mr Dry-Bone (after all, he eventually 'wins' Miss Louise), and go on to position the other characters – animals and Miss Louise – as they think fit. Ensure that the children justify their placements (which should not be based on their own character preferences!).

- If they have been reading a tale in which some relationships to the main character/s seem closer than others, get children to draw several concentric rings on a piece of paper. Ask them to put a character sketch or coloured cross in the middle to represent the main character/s. They should then lightly stick sketches or different-coloured crosses representing the other characters where they feel appropriate on the diagram: characters' closeness to the centre depending on children's opinions of their closeness to the main character/s. (This activity could also be undertaken by dragging symbols around concentric rings on an interactive board.) In some texts, relationships may shift in closeness. For example, in Francesca Simon's *Don't be Horrid, Henry*, Henry's antagonism to his baby brother has moderated by the end. In this kind of case, pick certain points in the text and check with children whether their placement of the 'other characters' on the diagram remains appropriate. From stories where relationships are not only with the main character, simply ask children to group character sketches or colour-coded crosses on a blank piece of paper: close together if to them relationships seem close, widely spaced if not. For instance, if they have read Kenneth Grahame's *The Wind in the Willows* (available in picture-book and abridged editions), you would expect them to place Mole and Ratty in especially close proximity. Whatever the method used, ensure that children justify their 'constellations'.

- Equally, children can use a simple grid to compare and contrast features within one text, or across several. Invite them, in pairs or groups, simply to compare and contrast orally, using the headings in the grid as prompts. Alternatively, ask them to fill in each box with their ideas. (See Figures 2.1, 2.2 and 2.3.)

  This works with non-fiction, poetry or fiction. In a story, children can compare and contrast characters' personalities and behaviour, for example those of the industrious little red hen and the other animals in a version of the traditional tale. In Judy Allen's non-fiction text, *What Is a Wall, After All?*, they can tease out many differences and similarities in the techniques of wall-building illustrated and described. Looking 'across' texts, the underlying message of *The Boy Who Cried Wolf* and Phil Roxbee Cox's *Don't Tell Lies, Lucy!* is the same, but there are many differences in events, characters and settings. Children could equally compare and contrast different published versions of *Hansel and Gretel*, or the Noah's ark story. If they study several titles in Watts Books' *Day in the Life of* series, they should discover subtle differences, such as the 'frieze' designed at the top of each book's pages. By considering the poems 'The House that Jack Built' and John Foster's 'Football Story' through a grid, children should spot their one important similarity – the 'Russian dolls' structure that 'builds up' one stanza, including it in the next – and the key difference in their patterning (the latter poem 'builds up' the beginning *and* end of each stanza).

DIFFERENTIATION

With all these 'comparing and contrasting' activities, encourage confident children to think independently; put unsure children in pairs or groups with trusted peers. If they are recording thoughts on a grid, ensure unconfident writers are with more confident children who can scribe for them.

Title of story text or texts..

	Characters [fill in details]	Settings [fill in details]	Things that happen [fill in details]	Words in the story, or things that the characters say [fill in details]
	• How they look, sound or smell • How they behave, talk and move	• How they look, sound or smell • Exactly where and when • How they make you feel	• Who does what • When in the story and why • What the story is about	• Who says what • When in the story and why
What is the same about them?				
What is different about them?				

Figure 2.1 Grid for comparing and contrasting aspects of stories. You can enlarge this, or choose one or two columns only

Title of non-fiction text or texts...............

	Part of the text or the whole text [fill in details] • What it is about	Pictures • What kinds • What size and how many • Where they are on the page	Headings • How many kinds • What style and size • Where they are on the page	Text • What kinds • How much • Where it is on the page
What is the same about them?				
What is different about them?				

Figure 2.2   Grid for comparing and contrasting aspects of non-fiction. You can enlarge this, or choose one or two columns only

Titles of poems..........

	What it is about	The way it looks on the page	Where any rhymes are	Where any repeated words or ideas are
What is the same about them?				
What is different about them?				

Figure 2.3 Grid for comparing and contrasting poems. You can enlarge this, or choose one or two columns only

Sorting out

Ask children, ideally in pairs or groups, to distinguish any of the following sub-categories of text.

Words containing different phonemes

From a text read, ask children to sort words, for example, those whose '-ed' ending sounds /t/ as opposed to /d/; whose '-s' ending sounds /z/ as opposed to /s/; whose 'th' letter string sounds soft as opposed to hard; those containing silent as opposed to 'sounding' letters; or those that contain a long as opposed to a short vowel sound. One way of undertaking this activity is to supply children with suitable words from the text on individual cards. Once they have found each one in the text being read, they can sort them into two transparent pouches (postcard or photograph holders, available from any large stationer, useful for display).

Two kinds of sentences

From a text read, ask children to distinguish sentences with connectives from those without; sentences that issue instructions (using the imperative) from those that give information (written as statements); sentences of speech as opposed to narrative; or those in the past tense as opposed to those in the present.

Different kinds of text

From a collection of texts, ask children to separate fiction from non-fiction; traditional tales from stories in familiar settings; information (report) text from instructions; or recount from fiction (children will need at least two texts side by side). Alternatively, ask them to sort two elements within a text, such as the events or dialogue they consider more important from those they consider less so. (This is a valuable exercise, as it promotes effective summarising.)

In all cases, ask children to explain, and justify, their sorting. If necessary, they can record the groupings in two columns on a piece of paper or whiteboard; alternatively, they can drag the words, sentences or texts into columns on an interactive board. However, this should not be a writing-dominated activity.

DIFFERENTIATION

In all such activities, allow adventurous children, or those who could benefit from a challenge, to decide their own criteria for the groupings they make. For instance, provide a selection of texts, e.g. a range of stories, poetry or non-fiction, and ask them to think how to group them one way then another, finding as many different methods as they can. They should record these, for example as pictures or notes. Alternatively, isolate a range of words or sentences in a text, and challenge the children to sort them into two or more categories. They must, however, explain and justify these groupings to an audience. (If you have made the initial selection carefully, for example picking sentences with a large amount and variety of punctuation, or words that are all highly descriptive, the children's sorting is likely to be especially thoughtful.)

Solving puzzles, using clues

Many texts deliberately withhold information. Instead of being told characters' feelings and motivations, or having events explained in detail, child readers are invited to work things out for themselves. This is true of much quality fiction and poetry. Identify texts for children to read in which such 'information gaps' are there to explore. Then ask them the appropriate questions. For instance, explore any of the following sub-categories of question.

How do the characters feel?

Martin Waddell, in *Farmer Duck*, does not explicitly describe the web-footed hero's desperate weariness, nor does Lauren Child the mood of Lola or her relationship with Charlie in *I Will not ever never Eat a Tomato* and *I Am NOT Sleepy and I Will NOT go to Bed*; however, the clues of pictures, speech and events suggest some answers.

Why did the character/s behave, or events happen, as they did?

Maurice Sendak does not explain, in *Where the Wild Things Are*, why Max finds himself in a strange place and plays with the wild things; however, the way he has behaved at home offers some explanations. Likewise, Mairi Hedderwick's *Katie Morag* stories often leave an explanation unoffered, or a secret untold, as to how things have come about.

Who was it?

Some stories challenge readers to work out who has just 'entered the text', or performed certain actions. In *The Lighthouse Keeper's Tea*, Ronda and David Armitage leave children to deduce by 'reading between the lines' that the impressive surfer and Mr Grinling are one and the same; in Pamela Allen's *Who Sank the Boat?*, the answer to this question (the mouse) lies in the pictures, and – obliquely – in the words.

How did the character/s do that?

In Marjorie Newman's retelling of *Rabbit's Trick*, she does not spell out the fact that Rabbit absents himself from the tug-of-war, setting it up instead between Hippo and Elephant, nor that they are fooled into thinking that Rabbit is strong because they can't see each other. Again, readers must 'fill in the gaps' and 'read' the pictures.

Ask children to justify their answers to questions such as those above. They should back up their ideas by referring to the 'clues' in the text: precise wording, or details of the illustrations ('I know because of . . .').

DIFFERENTIATION

Leave such questions open for confident 'reading detectives'; however, give unsure 'reading detectives' a choice of answers, e.g. 'How does Farmer Duck feel here? Excited, sad, worn out or frightened?' 'How did Rabbit do the trick? Did he wind the rope round the tree, pull it really hard, get big animals to pull from each end, or ask some animals to help him pull his end?' They should still try to justify their chosen answers unaided, though. ('Looking for the clues' will prompt them to revise their first ideas if they are mistaken.)

Exploring dilemmas

Stories, non-fiction recounts and narrative poems often describe characters or real-life people in difficult situations. In Sue Heap's *Let's Play Fairies!*, Lily May needs a way of persuading her friends to leave their fantasy games and play hers. In the Chinese folktale *The Magic Paintbrush*, available in various editions, the boy with the brush whose paintings magically become real has the problem of escaping from the wicked emperor. Eli Francis's short non-fiction text *Survival* describes, amongst other scenarios, how two friends were trapped in an avalanche. Elizabeth Lang's poem 'Honey Bear' presents a bear who couldn't save money.

Ensure that some texts your children read present them with such dilemmas. Ask them to stop reading at the point where the problem has been presented, and:

- brainstorm ideas for a practical solution, in pairs or as a group; they can then suggest their favourite option;
- individually, draw pictures illustrating their preferred solution;
- question and advise an adult in the 'hotseat' (as the person in difficulties) about what they might do; or
- role-play the situation themselves, exploring what might best – or perhaps most originally – resolve things.

Stress that you are not asking children to 'second-guess' what happens in the original text, but to be independent-thinking, practical or imaginative. However arrived at, children's solutions must 'fit' the details of the words and illustrations, and the general 'mood' of the text. Afterwards, the rest of the text should be read. Ask children to discuss whose solutions to the dilemma they favour – one of their own or the author's.

DIFFERENTIATION

Leave the solutions to dilemmas open for confident children; however, support unconfident children by suggesting a few solutions yourself, some practical, others that do not fit the details of the scenario, and some unworkable. Encourage them to criticise and select from your examples.

Creative thinking

What could be the question with this answer?

These activities can be used for summative or formative assessment if desired. Give children just one of these 'answers':

- Capital letters.
- The letter/s – [fill in the blank, e.g. 's', 'k', 'e', 'ou'].
- Alliteration.
- A sentence.
- Dictionaries.
- The author/poet/illustrator – [fill in the blank: someone with a substantial oeuvre, e.g. Lauren Child, Nick Sharratt, Helen Craig, John Agard].

Set them the task of deciding, through reading, what the 'question' could have been. Stress that there is *no right question*. The 'best' ones will be unlike other children's, and include some detail. Children need to design their questions through close scrutiny of one or more appropriate texts (e.g. if the 'answer' is 'capital letters', their texts should contain capital letters, used for a variety of reasons). Children should already have learnt about the concept contained in the 'answer', e.g. capital letters. They can work individually or in pairs, orally or in writing: whichever you feel will produce best results.

DIFFERENTIATION

The more texts supplied, and the more varied, the more open the task becomes. Challenge more able children to suggest their own 'answers', without offering them particular formats for these; however, for children who need more support, give them frames for 'answers' that are more closed than those suggested above, for example:

- They make the sound – [fill in the blank, e.g. /ai/, /ee/, /ie/, /oa/, /oo/].
- They have — syllables [fill in the blank, e.g. two, three].
- They are opposites.
- They are all unusual or interesting words.
- They are all — [fill in the blank, e.g. fiction, non-fiction, poetry].
- They are all — [fill in the blank, e.g. settings, evil characters, fairy-tale characters, fantasy settings . . .].

You can also limit the challenge by providing only one appropriate passage, sentence or text from which to research the question.

Finally, some children will benefit from 'oral frames' to help them word their final responses to this task. Verbalise them, or display them in the classroom, as appropriate. Some might be:

- What do [children must give their list] have in common?
- What is the same about [children must give their list]?
- In [name of text], what can you say about [children must give a list of words]?
- What do we call the — that has/have [children must give a list of text features]?
- Who often writes about/uses [children must give a list of typical characteristics]?

Imagine . . .

For this activity, the emphasis is on creative *reading*, so don't ask children to write. Instead, invite them to do their 'imagining' through either small world play, i.e. making and/or manipulating figures in a miniature setting; role-play, for instance rehearsal then performance to the class; oral brainstorming; or drawing pictures and then explaining them to someone. Decide whether this is best done in groups, in pairs or individually.

Some fruitful sub-categories of challenge are as follows.

. . . *your own text ending*

This works best with texts in which there is some 'build-up', whether of clues, or patterning of language or events, that cumulatively suggests a certain kind of outcome. (Examples include many traditional tales, from a variety of cultures; *A Dark, Dark Tale* by Ruth Brown; non-fiction texts of explanation or recount; or poems such as 'Ten dancing dinosaurs', by John Foster, based on 'Ten green bottles'.) Make sure the text is unfamiliar. Read, study or discuss it in whatever way you have chosen until you reach the final line, verse, episode or page. Conceal this. Invite children to design 'their' ending in detail. Explain that there is no 'correct' ending. Endings must, however, 'fit' all the text that has gone before (including the details and 'mood' of any pictures). Individuals or groups should endeavour to think independently.

. . . *more like this*

Do this when reading a text with potential to expand on a situation or joke, or invent new scenes (fiction and plays), verses (poetry) or 'fact panels' (non-fiction). In this case, study the whole text first. Then suggest additional content to children. Ask them to imagine the language needed, accompanying visual imagery, etc. For example, in *Peace at Last* by Jill Murphy, Mr Bear visits a succession of places about the house trying to sleep; children could add an imagined episode in a bathroom or a playroom. In a text with a minor character who never speaks, through discussion or role-play, ideas for his/her speech (e.g. in speech bubble form) could be inserted. In an information text, for example about trains, new details on a sub-topic, e.g. steam trains, might be included.

. . . *the unknown*

This works when studying a text in which an object, character or event is either not described or not illustrated. For example, the blurb alone of Sarah Hayes's *The*

Grumpalump, without seeing pictures and text, leaves plenty of scope for speculation about what the Grumpalump is. In Philippe Dupasquier's *Dear Daddy*, the absent father's life aboard ship is illustrated but not captioned, and his responses to his daughter's letters are not given. In Debi Gliori's *The Snow Lambs*, monochrome picture panels alongside the main story depict the trials of a sheepdog and a sheep, but without narration. In non-fiction texts, there are sometimes descriptions (e.g. of an animal, object or place) or explanations (e.g. of a process) without pictures. Having studied the 'partial' text, brief children in detail on how to imagine what they don't know. This could be through drawing, discussion or role-play. In order to imagine unillustrated factual accounts in non-fiction texts, you might invite children to make models.

Another take on this activity is to conceal the title of a poem or story, asking children to invent their own. The original title is unimportant: invite a vote on the top favourites – some of which the children might consider more imaginative than the actual title, when you reveal it.

. . . new words

Do this while studying a text containing 'nonsense language'. Supply children with consonants and/or consonant clusters and digraphs, and, separately, vowels and/or vowel digraphs (e.g. on 'mix-and-match' cards). Ask them to try out different combinations of these, thus inventing new words for the text being studied.

. . . it went

This works for any text of quality that the children have enjoyed, once it has been discussed or studied in detail. Ask children to choose and/or make five things to represent the text to the world, 'as if it had been lost for ever'. Examples of items are: one word or phrase from it; a picture, artwork or map, made by the children; a model of one character or object, also made; a quote – what someone in class said about it; a tiny fragment from one page (this can be photocopied). If desired, children can then show their artefacts and explain them to the class as if to children of the future.

DIFFERENTIATION

Note that the more texts supplied, and the more varied, the more open and challenging the task becomes. Give slower or less confident children one part of the activity or one small task only, e.g., freeze-framing one moment in a scene, rather than role-playing a whole episode; helping to make a model in a group; or inventing one new word.

Design a project on . . .

Even young KS1 children can design and organise a reading-based research project. Examples of themes for research include:

- non-fiction;
- a particular spelling pattern;

- a specific punctuation mark;
- words connected with a subject of special interest (the children's choice, or yours);
- the layout of sentences in different texts;
- captions, labels or signs;
- one genre of story, e.g. fairy stories;
- plurals, or
- connectives.

Ask children – in groups, in pairs or individually – to plan:

1 What they want to know about the topic.
2 What texts, websites and other resources they may use for their research.
3 How they will do research, sharing out any sub-tasks.
4 How they will document or present their findings.
5 How they will timetable the enterprise, in consultation with you.

It is often possible to continue the project at home.

Of course, designing a project also entails problem-solving; it is in devising a format in which to showcase the results, however, that creative thinking is required. Some options children might choose are:

- an interview or role-played TV programme;
- a captioned display;
- photographs or pictures;
- a talk or group presentation, with 'props' or illustrations; or
- a scrapbook of captioned examples.

DIFFERENTIATION

Challenge able, or potentially able, children to decide their own timetables, questions to research and/or resources; however, others will need your guidance on these, and closer monitoring of their progress. For uncertain children, you may specify particular questions to research, e.g. for the non-fiction theme: 'How many kinds can I find?', 'How do I know it is non-fiction?', 'What are some differences from fiction?'; or for the spelling pattern 'kn' (silent *k*): 'How many words can I find with the pattern?', 'Where in words does it come?', 'Are there any other letters in words that can be silent?' To help further, you may stipulate and/or provide the books and websites to be used to research the theme. Finally, do not limit the choice of formats (above) in which children can present their findings, except for the least able (do not, however, *dictate* just one: even for them this would curtail the 'creative thinking' element).

After the children's presentations, you may wish to study the chosen theme further with the class.

Think again . . .

. . . from another viewpoint

This will require a text that includes (or suggests to you) more than one point of view. Thus a story, play or narrative poem will have minor characters experiencing events differently from the central figures. Many non-fiction texts convey a particular attitude, e.g. the interesting nature of spiders (while an alternative view is that they are scary).

First ensure that your initial study of the text with the children includes an awareness of the predominant outlook on the content, e.g., one character's, or the author's. Select another character or characters from the text if it is fictional. Posit people or characters who might hold another opinion in the case of non-fiction, e.g. in the example above, the flies that a spider catches and eats (who would find spiders scary). Through role-play and/or hotseating, ask children, in groups or as a class, to explore either events as they might have seemed to other characters (in fiction) or the new point of view on the subject-matter (in non-fiction). Use costumes, props or name stickers to keep children in role.

If desired, this can go further. For example, if working with narrative, children can go on to draw story maps, still in role as the alternative character/s, recording which events they would have witnessed, which settings they would have passed through, etc. If working with non-fiction, children can 'orally rewrite' the original text from the new, fictional person's perspective, i.e. still in role, rehearse and prepare an oral presentation of the text in a revised form, using the existing words as a prompt. Do not ask children to write: these activities are intended to encourage creative *readerly* responses.

. . . of the alternatives

Use a text the children are studying: either a fiction text in which a character makes choices or decisions, or a non-fiction text where the layout and design is distinctive or the content highly selective (e.g. a party recipe book with several traditional recipes, such as jelly, omitted).

Invite children to brainstorm – in pairs or groups – either:

- all the choices the decision-making character could have made, what might have happened as a result, and how that might have changed the story (in the case of fiction); or

- how else the designer and publisher could have laid out and designed the text (in the case of non-fiction); or

- what other themes or content could have been included (in the case of non-fiction).

Where children have brainstormed in pairs, invite them to 'snowball' next, i.e. to gather in fours to share their ideas. In these larger groups, ask them to negotiate their pooled alternatives down to a maximum of three top favourites – the choices *they* would have preferred. A copy or copies of the text can be put on display, with the children's preferences recorded as captions around it.

DIFFERENTIATION

In the first version of this activity, ensure that more confident role-players help others, rather than dominating them; you may need to intervene in uncertain groups' role-play with directive questioning. Ensure an adult is working with children in *small* groups for either version, if they are unclear about the activity. Be precise in your briefing, and model appropriate ideas: for instance, 'Think of a list between you of all the places she could have gone instead of into the woods, and what might have happened. For example, she might have gone over the hill, but then a bull might have butted her. Or she might have reached a castle, but then a knight might have charged out and frightened her.'

Bring together . . .

Children can work in pairs or groups for the various sub-categories of this activity.

. . . *features of fiction*

Pick a feature that children can search for and compare across different texts, for example: types of weather; witches; fantasy settings; wishes; losses; foreign lands; reasons for characters' arguments; spacecraft; words on a theme, e.g. connected to size ('big', 'vast', 'tiny') or shape ('lumpy', 'round', 'pointed'). Brief them to collect as many examples as they can from different sources, e.g. by bookmarking them in books or circling them on photocopied pages. Ask them what they have learnt about the range of options that authors use. An extension of this is to invite children to invent a 'hybrid' of the feature studied, e.g. a new, mixed-up kind of weather, or new words describing shapes, drawing on parts of the existing words they have discovered.

. . . *aspects of poetry*

Pick an aspect that children can search for and compare across a variety of poems, for example: poem shapes and layouts; rhyme schemes (as long as children understand what these are); words with a particular ending (rhymes or otherwise); or a theme, e.g. animals, home life, journeys. Brief them to collect as many examples as they can from different sources. Ask them what they have learnt from finding such a variety of poems with this feature. An extension of this is to invite children to invent something new from what they have discovered: *not* to write a new poem (a writing activity) but, for example, to sketch their own design for a distinctive poem shape and layout and give it a title; to brainstorm nonsense words with the rhyming ending studied, i.e. all the rhyming words that *don't* exist; or, if they have studied a theme such as animals, to list which animals do not seem to be treated by poets.

. . . *information from non-fiction*

Pick a research topic (possibly one being studied anyway), for example, 'New Year celebrations'. Alternatively, set the children a research question, for example, 'What kinds of music do people around the world use to celebrate New Year?' Brief them to find information on this theme from as many sources as they can: books and/or websites, pictures *and* text; the more disparate the sources, the more challenging the task. They can bookmark useful pages, or circle relevant information, if downloaded or on photocopies. Then ask them to collate the information into some new (largely non-written) form, e.g. a demonstration, an oral presentation or informative drawings with captions. Children must be able to show that they have 'fused' their findings into this new product.

> ## DIFFERENTIATION
>
> All children will need several texts, so if necessary ensure more capable researchers support uncertain ones by establishing mixed-ability groups. Do not pre-select the texts children should consult, and their length, unless children have limited research skills. The challenge comes in asking them to choose and generalise from, or combine, the particular information found from several sources.

Critical thinking

Many of the activities described below can follow many of those described in the 'Problem-solving' and 'Creative thinking' sections of this chapter. Most can equally stand alone.

Rating and choosing

While reading, or using certain texts for reference, ask children to identify and rate (for example as first, second and third):

- in a word-book or dictionary, the 'top' letters of the alphabet – for example, on the basis of their frequency as the initial letter in words;
- from a recently read story or poem, the 'top' phonemes – again, on the basis of how often they occur; alternatively, depending on which the reader liked best;
- the 'top' words, phrases, lines or sentences in any newly read piece of prose or poem – for instance, on the basis of which seem to 'stand for' the text best;
- the most interesting, surprising or unusual facts;
- the 'top' texts out of several (websites, magazines, non-fiction, fiction or poems) – for example, on the basis of which are most useful on a subject, or which are the most exciting or funny;
- the 'top' genres of story from a variety of examples recently read or a list provided, e.g. stories in a familiar setting, comic tales, fairy tales, fantasy stories, animal tales, stories from other cultures – perhaps based on readers' preferences;
- words, phrases or sentences of a recently read text, based on how hard they are to read or understand; or
- words, phrases, sentences, lines or passages of a recently read text on the basis of which are the children's favourites, or the reverse.

They can agree this 'ranking' through discussion in a pair or group, or decide it individually. Ask them to justify their preferences.

In further variants of this task:

- Ask children to rate their invented titles for a text whose original title you have concealed (an activity suggested in the 'Creative thinking' section): which is their preferred title, second favourite, and so on?

- Stop readers when they encounter a difficult word whilst reading. Ask them to brainstorm and rate the strategies they could use (reading back, reading on, breaking down phonically, looking for known letter strings, guessing from the first sound in the word, guessing from the context and/or pictures, etc.): which is likely to be the most effective, the next-most effective, etc.?

- Invite individuals to rate and discuss their own 'reading performances' during several recent occasions of guided or group reading.

Alternatively, children can identify their number one choice. Urge them to justify its selection.

In another variant, ask children to use a 'Comparing and contrasting' grid, similar to Figures 2.1–2.3 in the 'Problem-solving' section (pages 45–7), to show their preference of one text over another. In place of 'What is the same about them?' and 'What is different about them?', substitute the headings, 'What do you prefer from one text?' and 'What makes it better, for you, than the other?'

DIFFERENTIATION

Invite adventurous thinkers and readers to do one of the above rating activities using a criterion of their own, e.g. favourite, least favourite, funniest, most boring, hardest, longest, shortest, most heavily punctuated, most frequent, most surprising, most unusual.

Recommendations

At least initially, ask children to practise reading recommendations orally, e.g. by turning to a partner or addressing a group (written reviews are primarily a writing, not a reading, challenge). Where possible they should make them to a motivating audience, such as a friend who does not know about the recommended 'item', a reading buddy from another class or children in role (e.g. as illiterate aliens from another planet!). Some ideas for recommendations are:

- the 'top three' – or one – chosen item/s from the 'rating and choosing' list above;

- a favourite subject in non-fiction (e.g. cars, ponies);

- a preferred method of selecting reading books; or

- tips for reading aloud a particular text or type of text, e.g. a rhyming or comic poem, a story or passage of dialogue, or an information book.

Ensure that readers explain *why* they are making their recommendations.

> ## DIFFERENTIATION
>
> Ask readers who need an extra challenge to play devil's advocate sometimes, i.e. perhaps to find three 'good things' to recommend even in a genre, text or passage they do/did *not* enjoy. Suggest to children who need support such speaking frames as 'You would really like/enjoy . . . because', 'The special thing about *x* is . . .' or 'The reason I chose *x* is . . .' Rephrase your questioning if children find 'Why?' questions hard. Ask instead, '*What* do you like/find exciting, special, helpful, etc. about *x*?' (This directs readers to list or quote specific aspects of their reading.) If they are recommending a text, or part of one, it may help if they describe three important parts of, or events in, that text first.

Polarities

Having read a text or a self-contained part of one (e.g. a chapter), give the children a pair of opposing value-judgement words, such as:

- good/bad;
- like/dislike;
- agree/disagree;
- easy/difficult; or
- right/wrong.

Challenge them to use these words to make statements about *either* the layout, characters, actions, events, other aspects of the text, such as the author's choice of words, *or* their own reading performance. They must justify their statements with reasons or details, for instance, 'I think Cinderella's step-sisters were *bad* because they were mean and would not let her go to the ball', or 'I *agree* that some animals should be kept in special safe places if there are few of them left in the world because that way maybe they will have more babies and survive.' Encourage children to make statements that are different from others they have already heard.

> ## DIFFERENTIATION
>
> Give confident thinkers several of the above pairs of words, for example, shuffled up on separate cards. Invite each child to pick one; challenge them to make a statement using their selected word, even though this may prove hard, e.g. 'I *disagree* with the author for using the word "big" because "enormous" would be much more interesting.' Direct more closed questions at uncertain thinkers, e.g. 'Who do you think was *bad* or *good* in the story, and why?', or 'Which words did you find *difficult* or *easy* to read or understand?'

Evaluations

Three sub-categories of this approach are suggested below.

Giving opinions

Whilst or after reading a whole or part of a text, ask children *either* what they think of, *or* how they would describe:

- particular words or phrases;

- certain sentences or lines;

- selected characters, or those characters' speech or behaviour, in stories;

- the text layout, especially with non-fiction (use of space, style of fonts, positioning of pictures, sub-headings, captions, etc.);

- their own 'reading performance'; or

- their performance in one of the reading activities described in the 'Problem-solving' or 'Creative thinking' sections of this book.

One approach is to ask each child for a 'snap judgement' on this in one or two words initially (you may wish to jot their ideas down); then to discuss the 'item', e.g. a particular character, in more depth, with reference to the reading and the text; finally, to invite them to revise their initial impressions (recording any changes). Praise readers who are prepared to adjust those first responses. Ask them *why* (in other words, *what* made them change their views).

An alternative approach is to select one appropriate aspect listed above and to ask:

- 'Did you like it/them? Why?'

- 'Did you understand it/them? Why?'

- 'Did you find it/them funny, interesting, difficult, surprising, etc? Why?'

Also, periodically ask them about themselves as readers:

- What do they consider their strengths and weaknesses?

- What do they like or dislike reading?

- Are there types of text they avoid, or read in large amounts? Why?

- How hard do they find it to read alone, and for how long, with concentration? Why?

- What do they feel about reading aloud as opposed to reading silently?

- Do they prefer reading with others or alone, at home or at school, in a quiet or a busy place? Why?

Jotting down their responses – or asking them to, for example in a reading journal, see page 61 – provides invaluable information about children as readers; it also heightens their self-awareness about their reading (metacognition).

DIFFERENTIATION

If inviting opinions, give confident children an open, unguided choice of responses but uncertain children a more limited choice. For example, when asking them to evaluate their own reading, invite them to choose between descriptions such as 'improving', 'unsure', 'quiet', 'full of expression', 'confident', 'fluent', 'self-correcting', etc. Where readers struggle to explain *why* they liked or disliked a text or found it hard to understand, ask them instead to explain *what* they liked, disliked or found difficult.

Judging

After you or the children have read a text or a self-contained part of one (e.g. a chapter), ask them whether:

- they would keep it in or out of a small 'reading suitcase';
- they liked or disliked it (and how much, e.g., on a scale, 1 to 5);
- they found it boring or entertaining/interesting (and how much, e.g. on a scale);
- they thought it was funny (and how funny, e.g. on a scale);
- it held any surprises;
- it made them want to hear/read more (of the text, in the same genre or vein or by the same author);
- they found it hard to follow/read (and if so, how hard); and/or
- they liked or disliked your/their own 'reading performance' (and how much).

Ask children for a show of hands, yes or no, on each discussion point, or undertake a 'secret ballot' on pieces of paper. Welcome diverse responses: celebrate non-conformity. Over a period of time, you may wish to build up a star rating system for texts read in a group or class, using some of the criteria above.

Jotting down their responses – or asking them to, for example in a reading journal, see below – provides invaluable information about children as readers; it also heightens their self-awareness about their reading (metacognition).

DIFFERENTIATION

Asking children to give their opinions (the earlier section) is more open-ended and thus more challenging than inviting their judgements against a criterion of your choosing (this section). Challenge more able speakers to decide their own vocabulary when judging; however, for children who struggle to find useful vocabulary, suggest words of different 'intensities' matched, say, to the numbers 1 to 5 in a scale; for instance, if inviting them to judge the humour of a text, introduce them to a spectrum of terms ranging from 'droll' to 'amusing', to 'witty', 'funny' and 'hilarious'.

Reading journals

Ask confident reader-writers to keep journals in which to record their judgements and opinions of their reading (perhaps using existing home-school diaries, or thinking/learning logs). In order to promote thoughtful, critical entries, insert in these, ready for use, a list of generic questions, for example for fiction:

- Describe a character: why does he/she stand out in your mind?

- Describe a setting: what does the author make you feel about it, and how?

- Choose an event that you found exciting, funny or surprising: why?

- Which three sentences or phrases did you like best? What did you like about them? What did they make you feel?

- List any words you did not know or found hard. How did you work them out?

- After your reading, write down what you think might happen next. Next time, record how close your prediction was. What, if anything, surprised you?

- What kind of book/text is this? Does it remind you of any others, films, TV programmes, etc? What do you like or dislike about it so far?

And for non-fiction:

- How much did you know about this subject before reading? What would you like to find out? By the end of this read, did you?

- What do you think of the design and layout?

- Has your read taught you any new words or phrases? What do they mean?

- Which parts of the text, if any, did you find hard? How did you work them out?

- Try looking three things up in this text. What did you search for? How easy is it to find your way around?

Ask children when they are reading independently, for instance at home, to choose one of these 'items' and respond to it in writing. Alternatively, select an 'item' for them. You might like to add a final question to the lists above:

- How easy do you find it to write about your reading? What do you find hard?

Again, this focuses on metacognition.

> ## DIFFERENTIATION
>
> For confident reader-writers, this is an excellent activity to bridge school *and* home reading. For children unfamiliar with keeping a reading journal, you will need to model writing entries yourself in class, expressing your personal observations on texts you have read recently. If you wish to give the unconfident a chance to try simple entries, again do so in class, and provide them with writing frames, such as 'What I liked about [name of character] was . . .', 'Some new things I found out were . . .'.

What to do differently?

After reading a text to or with children, ask them:

- what the author could do to make a particular character (or events) funnier, more interesting, more or less frightening or less predictable;

- how the writer could make his/her language more unusual, interesting, descriptive or beautiful to listen to;
- in what ways the layout of a text, the pictures, a book cover or blurb could be made more attractive or easier to follow; or
- how the reader/s could improve their 'reading performance' next time.

> ## DIFFERENTIATION
>
> Invite able children to caption the text with their suggestions, e.g. for a classroom display; alternatively, to incorporate their suggestions into a letter to the author or publisher of the text. With the less able, jot down their thoughts on their behalf, e.g. their responses when you ask them to consider improvements for a future 'reading performance' of their own. Remind them of these notes before the next similar reading begins, encouraging them to evaluate this next performance in the light of their ideas.

How was it?

Before they begin to read any text not previously seen, prime children to be alert to:

- how they feel when they first see the text and know they are going to read it;
- in the case of a story, what they think when they encounter the first character, setting or event;
- in the case of non-fiction, what they think or do when they encounter facts and features (e.g. 'did you know?' panels or fonts) they didn't expect;
- how they react if faced with words they don't know; and/or
- whether they feel differently, or are surprised, as they read more.

After the read, ask them to relate to you or peers these feelings and impressions (metacognition). Praise readers' honesty, and especially their readiness to reveal different responses from those of their peers.

> ## DIFFERENTIATION
>
> If reading independently, confident reader-writers can note their various reactions in a reading journal (see page 61). While studying a common text, they might read their entries aloud to their group.
>
> Ask less confident readers to feed back – perhaps orally – on only one or two of the points above. Alternatively, ask them to sticker with Post-it® notes the points in the text where they encounter the first character, setting, event, unknown fact, unexpected feature, surprise or difficult word (label these in advance if you like, e.g. 'A word I don't know', 'A surprise in the layout'). They can record on each sticker (or tell you later) how they reacted at these points, e.g. 'I looked up the word in a dictionary', or 'I didn't know which words to read next.'

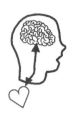

Affective thinking and emotional literacy

Tracking thoughts and feelings . . .

In a range of learning contexts, draw children's attention to the wide variety of human emotions: anger, fear, happiness, sadness, anxiety, disgust, surprise, like, dislike. . . . Consider together the differences in people's body language and behaviour when experiencing each feeling, and the kinds of situations that provoke them. (Avoid labelling some emotions as 'good', others as 'bad'. Stress that all feelings are valid in certain contexts; promote the importance of recognising and managing them well.) You may find it useful collaboratively to devise an emoticon (a simple facial expression symbol representing an emotion) for each feeling discussed; display them somewhere, for instance on a poster, for classroom use in a wide range of learning contexts. The following sub-categories of approach allow you to build on such work.

. . . through fiction or recount

Undertake this activity having read a fiction or recount text in which the feelings of one or more characters change, and in which these changes are either described explicitly or can be inferred. Invite children to record such fluctuations, using either a set of class emoticons or some of their own devising. They may append these to the text, on ready-made 'emoticon stickers' or having drawn them on Post-it® notes; alternatively, they can draw or stick emoticons in a sequence on a blank piece of paper, shadowing, as it were, the 'emotional shape' of the text.

DIFFERENTIATION

Give emotionally mature children opportunities to design their own emoticons, for example tracking in parallel the 'emotional journeys' of Sarah, Percy and Bill, the three *Owl Babies* from Martin Waddell's classic picture book. Mature thinkers can also be challenged to investigate texts whose characters are notably unlike themselves: adults, personalities with problems outside the children's own experience, etc. Encourage them to speculate on these more 'foreign' emotions – expressing their ideas via emoticons, role-play, writing or discussion.

With confident readers, encourage them to consider the 'whole read' in one sweep; however, with less certain readers, break the read into stages. Ask them to record the emotions of the characters as they occur using emoticons from a ready-prepared 'bank'. Thus they will still complete an overview of the 'emotional journey' described in the text. (Alternatively, ask the unconfident children to record the emotions from one part of the text, or of one character, only.)

After any such reading activity, encourage children to share and compare similar experiences and emotions they have known in their own lives.

. . . through metacognition

This expands on the 'How was it?' activity in the 'Critical thinking' section of this chapter (page 63). Before a reading task, prime children to stay alert to what they are thinking, and how they feel, throughout the task. Afterwards, ask them to describe these thoughts and feelings, for example, what, if anything, about the task made them anxious? How do they feel about these kinds of tasks or texts? Did anything remind them of another similar task or text? What did they feel about different aspects of the text? What did they think about their own or others' contributions to the reading, or the task? You might find a way of recording these impressions, e.g. list your questions down the side of a board and note each child's responses in a separate column. Now refine their observations in one of two ways:

1 Invite children to review their responses, distinguishing which were thoughts and which were feelings; for example, they might colour-code the notes into these two categories. (Debate the difference carefully.)

2 Ask children to review their responses, as if wearing *either* a red hat® (for their feelings and their thoughts) *or* a blue hat® (for their *thinking about* their feelings and their thoughts). As an example, children might have read a few pages from an information book about fireworks. Invited to review their impressions, one child might 'wear the red hat®' to repeat her recorded comment, 'I thought that the next page would be more history of fireworks, but it was about different kinds of fireworks.' 'Donning the blue hat®' she might gloss this: 'But that was probably because I really liked the history part and I wanted it to go on. Now I see that each double-page spread is about a new thing, so I should have realised that there wouldn't be more history over the page.'

DIFFERENTIATION

Both approaches outlined above are challenging, the second arguably more so. If children find these hard, revert to the simpler 'How was it?' approach described on page 63.

Risk-taking

Openly discuss, and value with readers, their ability and willingness to take risks; stress that risk-taking, i.e. trying unfamiliar things, is the only way learners learn. Challenge children sometimes to be 'brave enough' to make a choice or take a risk they would prefer not to. One approach is to designate the occasional reading session as a 'risk day'; alternatively, challenge unconfident children to join a 'risk group' or go to a 'risk area', e.g. a reading corner with that title, once every week or fortnight. Some examples of risk-taking in reading are to:

- guess words from the context (beginnings and ends of sentences, layout, pictures, etc.), *not* just attempt them from 'sounding out';
- choose unknown reading books, not just the familiar and oft-read;
- try a 'shunned' type of text, e.g. poetry, fiction, non-fiction, unillustrated;
- attempt a text on an unfamiliar subject;
- try to read silently instead of aloud;

- practise a 'performance read'; and
- share a text with a different reading group or partner.

> **DIFFERENTIATION**
>
> These approaches cut across the usual boundaries of 'able' and 'less able'. Many children, in both groups, need encouragement not to 'play safe' in their reading.

Boosting independence in 'early finishers'

Sometimes individual readers, or an unsupervised group, complete a reading task both successfully and earlier than expected. Identify any children who do so on a regular basis; encourage them in such situations not to come to you but to choose one from a bank of generic 'follow-on tasks', explained briefly on laminated index cards in a box somewhere accessible. Typical tasks can be:

- Find another text or book which has something in common with this one: the layout, some words, some facts, a character or type of character, a setting . . . . Think what is the same and what is different.

- Write down your three favourite words/phrases/lines/sentences (or stick a Post-it® note beside them). Decide what it is you like about each one.

- Find three words that were hard to read or understand. Write them down (or stick a Post-it® note beside them). Find a word book, dictionary or encyclopaedia that tells you more about them.

- Think of something new you would like in the text: a new section or event, more facts, a new character or picture that would make it even better. Where would it be? How would it be written or designed?

> **DIFFERENTIATION**
>
> This approach fosters 'early finishers'' independence of action and 'learning stamina', one aspect of affective thinking, while helping them to consider their reading more deeply. Note that these ideas apply only to 'able children', and only to those who work speedily (some able children work slowly and methodically).

Ideas from earlier sections

Taken from previous sections, the following sub-sections describe ideas that particularly promote affective thinking and emotional literacy.

Problem-solving

- Tracking the changing mood or behaviour of a character in a story, for example by making flick books (page 40), helps children to think about and identify their and others' feelings and motivations. Comparing or contrasting – or comparing *and* contrasting – characters from fiction is also useful: it highlights the existence of a wide variety of relationships and motivations, and the diversity of people's emotions and behaviour, for instance through activities such as drawing 'hierarchy trees' (page 43) or completing grids (page 44).

- If you are working on self-esteem issues with children, get them to compare and contrast fictional characters with 'self-image problems', such as Anthony Browne's *Willy the Wimp*, with the behaviour, speech and personalities of characters brimming with self-confidence, such as Ian Falconer's effervescent pig Olivia. Ask them to compare the courage of characters who 'dare to be different' with their conformist fellows, such as David Martin's *Little Chicken Chicken* and her feathered friends.

- 'Solving puzzles, using clues' advocates exposing children to fiction in which characters' feelings are not explicitly stated or their behaviour not directly explained (page 49). Allowing young readers to work these aspects out for themselves not only heightens their awareness of fictional characters' emotions and motivation but, if cross-referenced to real-life situations in which people's feelings are hidden, can foster their ability to make similar inferences about real people and situations. It also promotes an awareness that reading requires thought, i.e. independent effort.

- Under 'Exploring dilemmas', it is suggested that children debate or role-play how characters from fiction or non-fiction might resolve their difficulties (page 50). Once more, children should make 'real-life transference': give them the chance to share analogous experiences of their own, and to consider what they did, or would do, in similar situations.

Creative thinking

'Think again . . . from another viewpoint' (page 55) naturally throws the spotlight on others' thought processes and feelings. It also promotes empathy: children's ability to see situations, and the world, through others' eyes.

Critical thinking

- The 'Recommendations' approach (page 58) asks children to champion their own reading preferences, no matter how at variance with their peers'; it exposes them to the varied tastes of others, and encourages them not to feel afraid of being different.

- 'Polarities' (page 59), and the opinion-giving and judging activities described under 'Evaluations' (pages 59–61), also encourage differing viewpoints, plus the tolerance of those of others.

- If a group or pair decision is required for any of the 'Rating and choosing' activities described on pages 57–8, this stimulates the development of children's interpersonal skills: their abilities to listen to and appreciate others' ideas, lead or include other group members, negotiate and, where necessary, compromise. The same is true of any other reading activity in which several children are required to produce a joint or single outcome.

Slotting approaches together

Many of the approaches described under 'Problem-solving', 'Creative thinking' and 'Critical thinking' – and in this section too – can be 'slotted together' to create a block of work, or an in-depth study of one or several texts, if desired. Each phase should take children's thinking about their reading to a new level. This in-depth work will help them to develop 'learning stamina', one aspect of affective thinking.

Questioning skills

In reading, just as in speaking and listening, get children to practise devising interesting and appropriate questions, beginning 'Who?', 'What?', 'When?', 'Where?', 'Why?' and 'How?' (It is common to have these questions displayed in KS1 classrooms, as oral prompts, in any case.) Using these words as 'question frames' steers them away from too often starting questions with 'Do/Does?', or 'Is/Are?' (which tend to narrow down information in reply to 'Yes' or 'No'!). However, be aware of the medium in which you ask children to formulate questions in response to their reading: if they do so verbally, they are implementing speaking and listening skills, but if they do so in writing, the demands on children's writing skills may disadvantage unconfident writers and skew the task towards a writing, and away from a reading, activity.

Oral formats

Interview formats invite oral practice with reading-related questions. Use the 'question frames' above. Some formats listed below inevitably duplicate those listed in the 'Speaking and listening' chapter.

Interviews
Ask children to:

- watch/listen to real or onscreen interviews with authors, or people in role as characters from stories or poems (hotseating); ask children to notice the 'best'/most interesting questions, dictate them for you to transcribe and display, and then perhaps categorise them, e.g. according to sub-topics covered, or whether they are 'Who?', 'What?', 'When?, 'Where?', etc. questions;

- interview 'amateur writers' (e.g. the school secretary, a governor or a visitor who happens to write – in the widest sense – as part of his/her job);

- interview professional writers, book illustrators, workers on newspapers/magazines or book publishers – in person, on webcam or via video conferencing; and

- question people (e.g. peers, other classes, teachers, family), for example, in a survey about reading, or while hearing book recommendations.

Written formats

The following sub-categories of format allow the written practice of reading-related questions.

Collections

While reading, ask children to note down questions they encounter. (Examples of books containing questions are given in the 'Questioning skills' section of the chapter on Writing, pages 93–4.) Invite analytical thinkers to group the questions they find into categories of their choosing; give unsure classifiers groupings of your own, e.g. 'Who?', 'What?', 'When?', etc. and 'Other'. The questions can then be displayed, under headings of the appropriate 'question words', on the classroom wall. Discuss or vote on which are the 'best', most interesting, most amusing, most unusual, etc. questions.

Written dialogues

Give children opportunities to:

- follow up on the study of an author, or a visit by a storyteller, author, book illustrator or maker, by writing to or emailing them with questions about themselves and their work (there are several websites and publications through which they can be contacted); or

- investigate a topic in any subject online by inputting questions to a search engine, or interrogating a specialist website through email to its 'Contact us' address.

DIFFERENTIATION

Provide able questioners with opportunities, while using the formats above, to sustain their interrogations: encourage them to investigate the answers they receive in more depth, using formulae such as 'Can you tell me more about that?', 'What do you mean?', 'How does that work/did that happen?', 'But didn't you just say that . . .?', etc. 'What/Which?', 'How?' and 'Why?' questions are more challenging to formulate than a 'Where?' or 'Who?' question, so encourage confident reader-writers to try these. Suggest they also supplement their 'What/Which?' questions with a noun or noun phrase, e.g. 'What kind of . . .?', 'What size?', 'Which character?', and their 'How?' questions with an adverb or adjective, e.g. 'How often?', 'How difficult?', 'How quickly?' The most ambitious can try beginning 'What if . . .?', 'Could you have . . .?', 'Would it be possible/better/difficult, etc. to . . .?'

Any 'question frame' such as these can be provided on a slip of paper to aid unsure or experimenting questioners. Give the least confident one or two of the easier prompt words (e.g. 'Who?', 'When?') at most.

What could be the question with this answer?

This approach, already described, also extends questioning skills: see the 'Creative thinking' section in this chapter, page 51.

PLAN-DO-REVIEW FORMATS: A CASE STUDY

The following example of a Reading activity was incorporated in a unit of work at Reception/Year 1 around alphabet books, alphabet friezes and simple dictionaries. The work developed creative thinking, problem-solving and critical thinking, in particular, and tried to ensure affective thinking. Lessons followed the useful and versatile sequence of 'plan-do-review', similar to that promoted by Belle Wallace in her TASC problem-solving wheel (see Introduction, page 4). They meshed with ongoing phonics work, learning about the alphabet and alphabetical order, and the teaching of handwriting (letter formation).

Expectations from the task

From different children the teacher hoped for the learning outcomes described below.

Learning objectives: All children to suggest a research method, and some to suggest interesting/practical details of a research method (creative thinking and problem-solving); all to achieve a sense of ownership of their research task and resources used (affective thinking); some to be able to infer concealed details of the alphabet books and other resources (problem-solving) – an objective planned later, in the light of discussions with the children, described below; and all to be able to state something they liked/disliked about a resource used, and/or – in the case of more advanced thinkers – why (critical thinking).

Background and preparation
This class was already following a structured daily phonics and handwriting programme via the *Jolly Phonics* commercial scheme (which is multisensory, and includes work on letter formation) and the DfES's *Playing with Sounds* and *Progression in Phonics* materials.

   Ten days ahead of the teacher's intended focus on alphabet books and materials, she pointed out the classroom's alphabet frieze on the wall and shared and read Posy Simmonds' *F-Freezing ABC* to the class. She then asked the children: 'What do you already know about alphabet books and friezes?' It turned out that many, including those children with English as an additional language, owned, or had had experience of, these. They were keen to share this knowledge. A few could already explain that while some such resources simply featured words beginning with certain letters, others included stories, rhymes or games based around each letter; one child mentioned word books or dictionaries as alphabetical texts; and many were aware that their pages or sections were normally in alphabetical order.

   The teacher asked if the children would like to plan some work on such texts themselves for a little over a week's time; if so, what would they need, what would they like to do, and how would they do it? Talk partners turned to each other to brainstorm ideas for a moment, then the teacher collected and recorded suggestions (creative thinking). Many wanted to find and bring in alphabet resources to study, but equal numbers wanted to create their own alphabet books or wall decorations. The teacher had anticipated this, and assured children that she would accommodate their interests (ensuring affective thinking). Of those who wanted simply to look at alphabetical texts, she queried how and what audience they could tell what they had found out (creative thinking and problem-solving). She also asked how lessons could allow for both reading and 'artwork-based' activities, and how aspiring resource-makers could avoid simply copying existing resources, which might be rather a dull exercise.

After brainstorming further, the children decided, by class vote, to do an exhibition of their favourite alphabetical texts, their chosen audience being soft toys in class, who could be invited to 'visit'. One creative thinker suggested that those wishing to generate their own alphabetical resources could avoid copying them by doing so sight unseen, guided only by clues from children who had had sight of them (problem-solving). Impressed by this suggestion – influenced, no doubt, by a recent Speaking and Listening information-gap activity – the teacher adopted it with alacrity! After she had pressed the class further about the practicalities of undertaking book study and artwork at once, some children suggested, and it was agreed, that they should all study some resources for a while, before the information-gap activity took place (problem-solving).

Over the next ten days, the children and teacher collected and brought in alphabetical resources from home, libraries and from around the school. As well as books and friezes, they included several unusual items: a framed hand-stitched sampler, children's alphabet jigsaws, a set of decorated magnetic letters, an alphabet mobile and several texts in other languages and scripts.

The first lesson (creative thinking and problem-solving)

Having gathered together a wide range of alphabetical texts, the teacher distributed them as follows to small groups of children:

- Less confident thinkers and readers were given a range of disparate resources with minimal reading required, e.g. a jigsaw, mobile, and some alphabet friezes and books with pictures but no words.

- Developing problem-solvers were given books and friezes, some based around words starting with each alphabetical letter, others including simple lines or sentences incorporating these letters.

- The most advanced problem-solvers and readers were given books in which rhymes, sentences and stories incorporated each letter of the alphabet; some children also had simple dictionaries/word books giving information about word meanings or spellings.

She asked those in each group keen to organise an exhibition to decide how they could find out about the alphabetical resources in front of them. After a brief discussion, it was decided by a class vote that children should study then group and label these resources (using 'emergent writing' and/or phonics), explaining their decisions afterwards (problem-solving). The teacher agreed, challenging the most adventurous thinkers to find *several different* ways of grouping the same materials (creative thinking). (For other children needing more guidance, she suggested that they group the materials depending on whether they included words or not; what style of lettering was used; or into themes, e.g. animals, humour, stories, transport.)

By the end of the lesson, each table of children had categorised their materials into at least two groups, and had 'written' labels for a display accordingly. During the plenary session, representatives from each table showed their labels and explained their decisions; the teacher meanwhile scribed legible, correct spellings on to their labels underneath their 'writing'. Groups of the most creative thinkers had come up with several ways of categorising their resources, e.g. old and new; *and* stories, rhymes, lists of words per letter and single words per letter; *and* according to the style of font used.

The second lesson (problem-solving)

The next day, the teacher paired up the children: a keen 'exhibition organiser' from the previous day with a child who wished to make an alphabetical resource. She asked the latter children to choose one of the alphabetical books or friezes (featuring single words, or letters only) that they would like to illustrate (one they had not previously studied). Each went on to nominate a particular letter of the alphabet. A parent helper then assisted them with collecting and preparing suitable art materials ranging from crayons and felt pens to paints, plus plastic or foam examples of the relevant letter shape where useful.

Meanwhile the teacher and an assistant encouraged the children's partners, from studying the relevant sections of the resources chosen, to decide what clues to feed them. Thus the adults:

- coached diffident problem-setters in how to word descriptions of pictures; locate elements on the page; describe size, colour and shape of letters, etc.

- guided developing problem-setters additionally in giving clues about subject-matter, e.g. if an owl was featured, 'There is a bird that hoots at night', etc.

- discussed with the most able problem-setters ways of describing the style of illustrations and letters too, e.g. 'soft/strong colours', 'swirly', 'black outlines', 'knobbly nose', etc.

Children then teamed up in their allocated pairs. The 'describers' fed their artworking partners clues and descriptions about their chosen letter page or section, showing them *only other pages or sections* of the chosen resources to help with the finished products! The three adults circulated, helped and mediated in disputes! The producers of the artwork were thus developing their problem-solving skills, as well as skills in listening and letter formation.

At the end of the session, pairs compared the artwork with the original materials: much critical thinking was generated, and consideration of why things had gone well or less so. (This activity was so popular that, by demand, a further, unplanned session was undertaken, in which the partners swopped roles.)

The third lesson (creative and critical thinking)

The next day, the groups composed in the first lesson set up their parts of the exhibition of alphabetical resources, complete with captions and labels, on different tables in the classroom. The teacher encouraged them to make these as attractive as possible: several children had ideas for props or decorative items to add, e.g. tissue-paper flowers and, in one case, the class globe to accompany a round-the-world alphabetical text. The teacher then helped them to add their own artwork, undertaken in the activity described above.

Each child then carried a soft toy around the 'exhibition', conversing with it about what s/he liked in the display (critical thinking). In a plenary session, as many toys as possible (via their carriers!) were invited to tell the class one thing they had liked – or disliked (they were reminded to consider each other's feelings, and especially to be constructive in their comments about artwork!). The maturest critical thinkers were asked *why* they liked or disliked what they did: by rewording this as '*What was it* you liked/disliked about . . .?', most such children could give an answer. Finally, the class was asked through a show of hands, on a scale of 1 to 10, how much they had enjoyed these various activities (again, critical thinking).

CHAPTER 3

Writing

Problem-solving

Writing – other than writing from dictation, or the pure copying of someone else's text – *is* a kind of problem-solving. It is a process of decision-making at all levels: about which ideas or facts to include; how to organise them, then how to sequence them as words; what punctuation and vocabulary to use; and more. The categories of teaching approach described below work specifically on children's ability to problem-solve (although at the same time, the freer they are to make their own choices, the more 'creative' the process). These approaches can be applied to many writing tasks.

Sorting ideas

Sorting is an analytical form of problem-solving that also requires creative thinking (thinking widely on a subject); the sub-sections below describe it in various forms.

Mind-mapping

Before embarking on a piece of factually based writing, for example a recount, a report or poems based on observation, give children the opportunity to mind-map what they know or remember about the subject. If this process is familiar to them, after some teacher modelling they can do it in pairs or individually – ideally on to small whiteboards or using pencils on paper, so that they can make alterations easily. If they are unsure, as a whole class or group draw up one large, displayed map – also on a wipeable board, to facilitate adjustments. The subject should be recorded at the centre, e.g. 'The talk we had about —', or 'Our street'. Ask children to remember details about the topic; these should be recorded in clusters at the ends of radiating spokes, each spoke labelled as a 'sub-theme'. For example, for the topic of 'Our street', sub-themes could perhaps be its houses, shops, street furniture and history. (Sub-sub-themes may also suggest themselves, branching off from the initial clusters of information.) If doing this yourself, children should help with what to write or draw, where to place notations on the map and how to label 'spokes' (which is where much decision-making takes place) – preferably making additions themselves. Be sure to add graphics; rehearse together accompanying mimes, actions, jingles, acronyms or jokes. In this way auditory, kinaesthetic and visual learning is combined (see Figure 3.1, a completed map for a recount). When

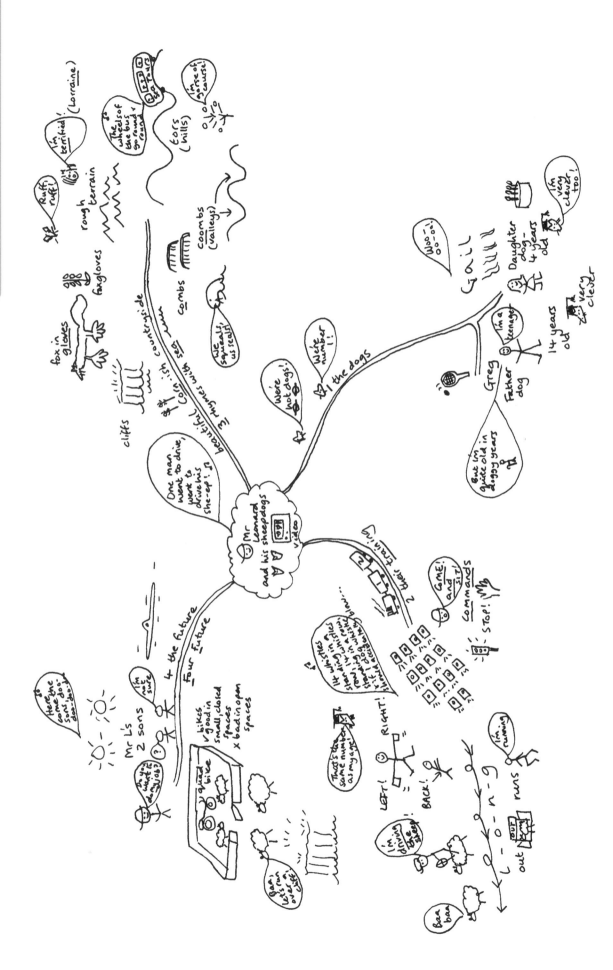

Figure 3.1 Mind map for recount of a video about a farmer and his sheepdogs

writing on the topic, stipulate the extent to which writers should use their map, for example, asking them to incorporate material from at least three 'branches'.

Before fiction writing, use mind-mapping as a way to brainstorm possible choices in the genre being written. For example, before writing stories in the familiar setting of a park, you might draw and label radiating spokes covering:

- 'settings within the setting', to which children might contribute, for example, a duck pond or the swings;
- 'typical characters', to which they might add a schoolchild, policeman or park-keeper;
- 'problems', such as losing something, an accident or bad weather; and
- 'some ways of sorting them out', such as getting help, using something in one character's possession or the arrival of someone new.

Allow children to suggest other spokes with different labels, depending on their concerns and interests. Subsequently, ask writers to choose one or two items from each spoke to incorporate into their stories.

Alternatively, focus in your mapping on the features of the genre to be written. Characteristics of traditional tales, for instance, might suggest spokes labelled:

- 'Typical settings'
- 'Typical characters'
- 'Traditional tales we know'
- 'Typical problems'
- 'Ways they are sorted out'
- 'Special words and language'

DIFFERENTIATION

Able thinkers can be challenged to complete their own maps, individually or in pairs (as long as they understand the method). With the less confident, use a concept map: instead of a blank with only the subject in the centre, begin with radiating spokes ready-labelled with headings ('concepts') – see Figure 3.2, a concept map for a poem. You might even give some examples of items at the end of each spoke. A whole-class or whole-group map undertaken with an adult in charge is especially supportive.

Sequencing

Sequencing the elements of all written texts presents children with decisions and problems. Where recall is involved – for example, when writing instructions for an activity having undertaken it, or a recount or review of actual events, or when rewriting a known story – choices about sequencing may be constrained but are still essential. (Sequencing becomes a 'puzzle', to be 'solved'.) If possible, ensure photographs are taken of anything actually experienced by the children. In cases such as retelling a known story, have pictures, sketches or symbols available of all

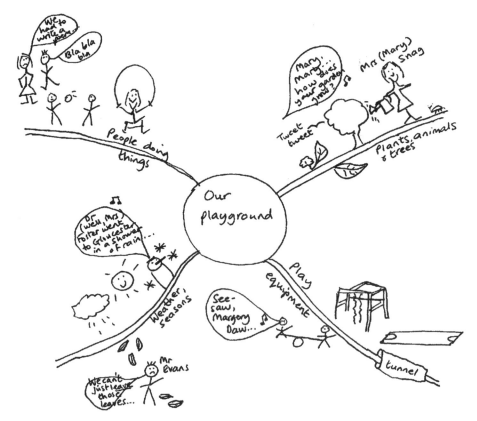

Figure 3.2 Concept map for a playground poem

the main events, or create them with the children's help. These separate illustrations, in whatever form, can be imported on to an interactive board, stuck to a class display board or large whiteboard, or provided to children in sets, like batches of pieces for a jigsaw. Whatever their medium, arrange the pictures in a random order to start with; then invite the children, in pairs, groups or as a class, to sequence them as best they can from memory – for example, by dragging them around an interactive board or sticking them in a line on to card (to create a storyboard).

Information (report) writing does not often require chronological recall; however, it still needs writers to decide on a suitable order for 'sub-topics' of the subject. Therefore, when preparing to write report text, a collection of pictures illustrating these 'sub-themes' also aids children (for instance, if children are to write about the fire service, pictures of firefighters' equipment, transport and duties). Sequencing is best done collaboratively, in order to encourage debate about the reasons for choices.

After the sequencing process, all writers can write to their 'comic strip' of illustrations, i.e. follow the sequence visually, allowing it to prompt and guide them in their prose.

DIFFERENTIATION

Challenge confident children to write more prose (e.g. several sentences) in response to each picture. For the initial sequencing of illustrations, ensure that children with memory problems are supported by peers with better recall. Alternatively, give them fewer pictures, and/or intersperse the task with discussion and feedback at each completed stage, praising good decisions. When it comes to 'writing up', help the easily confused to stay on task by revealing only one picture at a time (conceal all others in some way, e.g. by turning them face-down, until they are needed).

Making choices

Giving writers two or three choices, as in the three sub-categories of approach outlined below, again highlights the decision-making aspect of writing.

Support for individual writers

Allow all writers *some* scope for choice. Thus whenever you are supporting individuals, and they ask for help, always respond with *options* (probably giving these verbally): whether two or three ideas for content, alternatives in vocabulary (e.g. a choice of synonyms), suggestions for punctuation and where to place it, thoughts about sentence construction or possible spellings.

Group approaches

When teaching writing with a class or group, brainstorm some options with children, then record them as a reminder, ideally in words and memory-jogging sketches. For example, before writing a letter you might brainstorm ideas for two alternative text layouts. Ask children to choose one (suggest that more adventurous writers adapt one or invent their own, i.e. that they use creative thinking). As another example, if children are working on character portraits, you might first brainstorm useful adjectives and descriptive phrases and display them as a list, under such headings as 'Looks', 'Voice and sounds', 'Clothes', 'Personality', 'Likes and dislikes'. Then stipulate the minimum number of selections you wish children to make (again, the more adventurous may 'edit' displayed vocabulary and phrases or use their own).

Writing frames

Work with writing frames is a powerful introduction to decision-making. Begin with a model text: this might be a published example, or writing you are demonstrating yourself. Either way, its subject-matter should be analogous, but not identical, to what you expect from the children; for instance, if they are to write 'About our Arms and Legs', your model might be 'About our Senses'. Invite children to pick out wording – especially at the start of sentences – that can be 'recycled' in the text they are to write. This requires analytical thinking, and creative thinking too, if writers suggest adaptations to sentence constructions suited to the new subject-matter. (Some children find this hard, as it requires extrapolation and generalisation; however, repeated practice in different contexts eventually brings rewards.) Underline or highlight in colour the words that can be 'recycled' – see Figure 3.3. Rewrite these 'frames' and display them; now brainstorm and add ideas for further frames that could be useful. As children begin to write, stipulate the minimum number of displayed frames you wish them to use.

About our Senses

in   above
on   below

Our eyes are at the front of our heads. They are on our faces above our noses and under our foreheads. Inside them, there are lenses, nerves and muscles. Their important job is to see all around us. This helps us to understand what is happening in the world.

The way our ears are built and shaped helps us to pick up as many sounds as we can. Without them, we would not be able to understand so much of what is happening. We might have to use our other senses much more.

List of 'extrapolated' writing frames

Arms

- Our ⬚ are in/on/at the ⬚ of our
- They are above/below/on/our
- Inside them, there are
- Their important job is to
- This helps us to

Legs

- The way our ⬚ are built and shaped helps us to
- Without them, we would not be able to
- We might have to use our

Extra ideas, from brainstorming with the children (for 'Arms' *or* 'Legs' sections)

- Within our bodies, they are joined to
- With them, we
- We move them by
- Our ⬚ can ⬚ , ⬚ and

Figure 3.3   Creating writing frames for 'About our Arms and Legs'

This method can be adopted with poetry and fiction, not just non-fiction. Again, show (or demonstrate writing) a text with elements of wording that can clearly be 'recycled'. If modelling poetry, show lines with patterned language, e.g. 'Through the window . . .,/Through the window . . .,/Through the window . . .'. Children can brainstorm the new poems this pattern could suggest, for example pieces in which each line begins 'Through the mirror . . .', 'Through the keyhole . . .' or 'Through the fence . . .'. When story writing, explore a story with children in which they can find 'sentence frames' to reuse that either introduce a character, set a scene or narrate exciting events.

> ## DIFFERENTIATION
>
> Suggest more adventurous children use as many writing frames as they can, and adapt the wording of the frames if they would like. Encourage the most confident writers, in addition or instead, to invent some of their own. The more children adapt and invent, the more they are problem-solving in a creative way (see the 'Choose your own . . .' approaches described in the 'Creative thinking' section, page 82). Give unconfident children a limited choice of writing frames (these can be colour-coded in your display, so that they know which ones to select from).

How can you manage?

Limiting children's written content or writing resources, their 'writing palette' as it were, can present them with thought-provoking challenges. For those with a tendency to shapeless length or lack of clarity, it can also be a useful discipline. For instance:

- Restrict the number of story characters to two or three, of the writers' choice.
- Similarly, stipulate one story setting only, of the writers' choice.
- Bar dialogue in narrative.
- Limit the use of certain connectives, e.g. 'and', 'but', 'then' and 'so' – say to three times each. (Ensure writers are familiar with alternative ways of linking text, such as deleting overused connectives and starting new sentences instead. Make sure you have also modelled and practised writing using other connectives, and supply them with a list of these to remind them.)
- Confine children's use of proper nouns to a few times. (Make sure you have modelled and practised writing using pronouns, and supply them with a list to remind them of their usefulness as replacements.)
- Remove spelling aids, such as word books or high frequency word lists. Encourage writers to try all spellings as they go (whether on a 'have-a-go' pad or in their writing).
- Forbid the use of rubbers and erasing fluid. Point out that these destroy invaluable evidence of progress. Invite children to suggest alternative methods for when they make mistakes (e.g. neat crossing-out or brackets, both of which preserve a record of their thoughts).

The last four suggestions can usefully be applied to most writing tasks, and work best as a whole-school approach.

> ## DIFFERENTIATION
>
> In all cases, encourage able thinkers to suggest *why* you are imposing these constraints. Explain the benefits to the less aware.

Creative thinking

How many kinds of writing . . .?

. . . could there be in the role-play area or a small world?

Invite children, when exploring (or discussing) a role-play area or small world environment such as a dolls' house or playmat, to imagine what different kinds of writing might be needed in it, and – if they wish – to try these out while playing there. For example, different people in a health centre/doctor's surgery might keep a diary of appointments (in book or computerised form), annotate a calendar, take phone messages by hand, record information about each patient (in files or on computer), write or print out prescriptions, complete questionnaires, etc. Challenge children to come up with a long list orally, or to show you a great variety of writing tasks. This is often a useful springboard into detailed work on one particular kind of text, e.g. writing messages, as the interest and impetus will have come in part from the children themselves.

> ### DIFFERENTIATION
>
> Allow able thinkers the freedom to devise their own ideas. For the less able or experienced, showing them pictures or a video, e.g., of real doctors' surgeries complete with environmental print (index files, prescription pads, appointment diaries, magazines and such), can help inform their thinking.

. . . could there be behind a text?

While studying a story, play or narrative poem in detail, brainstorm with the children all the kinds of text that could be written incidental to the action. For example, Vivian French's *The Little Red Hen and The Sly Fox*, in which the fox steals the hen for his chicken dinner, could suggest: an advertisement for the hen's sewing and mending services; a map of the woods, with the various animals' houses annotated; labels on the hen's apron pocket, listing its contents; the fox's recipe for his chicken supper; and warning signs about the dangers of climbing on tall cupboards (which makes the hen dizzy) and cooking with boiling water (which scalds the fox). Challenge children to compete to come up with the longest list and the greatest variety of writing tasks. Once more, this approach is a useful starting-point for detailed work on one or more of the particular text types brainstormed.

> ### DIFFERENTIATION
>
> Leave able thinkers to brainstorm their own ideas, e.g. in single-ability pairs or groups. Give the less confident examples, or a list of possible types of print, to spark their thinking.

Insert . . .

Do this activity while studying:

- a sign containing several messages, e.g. an official notice in the school foyer;
- a collection of captions, perhaps those on a double-page spread, e.g. in an information (report) text on a subject being studied;
- a story with patterned language and/or events, e.g. Pamela Allen's *Who Sank the Boat?* or Simon Bartram's *Man on the Moon*; or
- a (non-rhyming) poem by a well-known poet, e.g. 'Trainers' by Michael Rosen.

It should have a distinctive style and tone, and possibly, in the case of non-fiction or poetry, a distinctive design or layout too.

Ask children to write (and possibly design the layout for):

- an extra message, in the case of a school notice;
- an extra caption or captions, in the case of a report text;
- an extra line of narrative or a short new episode, in the case of a story; or
- an extra line or two or a stanza, in the case of a poem.

They should imagine that it will be inserted in the middle of the original text (in a place located by you). The challenge is to make the writing sound as seamless with the original text as possible when read as part of the whole.

DIFFERENTIATION

Do not brief really adventurous, confident writers about the content; however, with many children you will need to specify the precise subject-matter of the new material (this aspect is not the main challenge). For example:

- An extra message for a school notice could warn readers to check that their shoes are not muddy before walking around school in them.

- An extra caption/s for a report text describing different kinds of weather could describe (from pictures) what people wear in various weather conditions.

- Extra narrative for *Who Sank the Boat?* could introduce a new animal and tell their part in the story; while in *Man on the Moon*, a new time added to Bob's work schedule could encourage children to narrate further lunar tasks he might perform.

- An extra stanza for 'Trainers', which demands the reader to 'See me in my trainers' – speeding in them in one stanza, kicking with them in the next – could describe the author abusing his trainers, employing them as containers, missiles, door-stops, hammers, etc!

This activity requires children to experiment with the subtleties of the original author/publisher's style, language and possibly layout; as such, it may not be suitable for a whole class. The least confident writers may need first of all to gain experience of writing that particular kind of text in general, possibly drawing on the studied text as their model.

Transformations

Begin with a shortish text that is rather bland in its language choices (e.g. 'saw', 'went', 'came', 'walked', 'got', 'said' in a story passage; or 'put', 'cut', 'cook' in instructions; or nouns qualified by few adjectives in report text). Sometimes an anonymised piece of writing from a past pupil is a useful model. Display it to the group or class on a board, OHP or screen. Invite children to help you edit the text to make it more descriptive and precise (e.g. replacing 'saw' with 'spotted', 'went' with 'escaped', 'came' with 'rushed in', 'got' with 'picked up', 'said' with 'whispered' in the story passage; or replacing 'put' with 'add', 'cut' with 'chop', 'cook' with 'bake' in the instructions; or by adding precisely descriptive adjectives in the report text). Encourage the children to cross out, replace and insert words ruthlessly.

Immediately afterwards, ask them – in pairs – to select a sentence or two from something similar they have written recently. Challenge partners to help each other imaginatively to improve these sentences with more precise and descriptive vocabulary. The group or class could vote on the most creative, unusual improvements.

DIFFERENTIATION

Many children will benefit from being paired with someone of roughly their own ability level, but whom they might not have chosen for themselves. If useful, draw children's attention to which sentences in their own writing are ripe for improvement by highlighting or marking them in some way before the session begins.

Choose your own . . .

While undertaking a particular writing task, some children find it stimulating to be allowed free choice of:

- subject-matter, e.g. for instructions, details of how to make *anything* they have made recently; for recount, an account of *any* lesson or activity they enjoyed recently;
- intended reader, e.g. a family member, a sick classmate, a pen-pal, a favourite toy;
- text layout, e.g. centred, justified right or justified left;
- font styles and sizes if writing on the computer; or
- viewpoint, e.g. if writing a version of *Cinderella*, from the perspective of a mouse, the slipper, the fairy godmother, the clock or an ugly sister; if writing up a museum outing, a recount from the perspective of the exhibits, the guide or the teacher.

DIFFERENTIATION

Give confident writers more options, or do not even specify any to them. Give less confident writers a limited number of options, rather than a 'blank canvas' of choice – for example, if you let them choose a novel viewpoint, give them just two alternatives (more problem-solving than creative thinking: see 'Making choices' in the 'Problem-solving' section, page 77). However, always allow writers the chance to suggest other possibilities that you may not have considered. Even risk-averse writers will benefit from such challenges, if set periodically. However, you may well need to model and demonstrate how the various options will 'look' on the page, and/or the conventions of the writing involved.

Imagine the words

Give children, individually or in pairs, either:

- a wordless picture storybook, e.g. *Little Star* by Antonin Louchard, or *The Great Escape* or *I Can't Sleep*, both by Philippe Dupasquier (the pictures may or may not be in 'cartoon strip' form);
- a double-page spread or so from such a book;
- a story or non-fiction text in picture-book format, with the words in a language not known to the children (feel free to give English text to children who have little or no experience of English!); or
- a highly illustrated story or information text with the words concealed, e.g. under Post-it® notes.

Ask them to write the words they imagine are necessary to 'tell the story of', or give the information in, the pictures: in the case of non-English-speaking children, in their own language if desired. Stress that you are not expecting some 'correct' version of the text, but are seeking insightful and imaginative responses. Challenge adventurous writers to come up with unusual and unexpected words and ideas that nonetheless 'fit' the illustrations.

DIFFERENTIATION

Give confident children a larger number of illustrations than you give unsure children; however many, the pictures must still potentially constitute a coherent 'whole', e.g. a very short narrative with a beginning, middle and end, or a complete recount. You may need to model some ideas of your own for a creative text that 'narrates' the illustrations before they begin; stress, though, that writers must develop their own ideas. Children who are inhibited writers, perhaps because of limited phonics or undeveloped handwriting skills, can still rehearse and refine a text orally, e.g. with a trusted peer or with an adult.

Alternatively, from a text that is already well known to them, give children the 'writing frames', i.e. the parts of lines and sentences in the text that are patterned or repeated – for example, Bill Martin Junior's classic lines, 'Brown bear, brown bear, what do you see? I see a [blank] looking at me'; these can be handwritten or printed on several otherwise blank sheets. (They motivate children more if presented as the pages of a book and bound or stapled, perhaps with a cover already inscribed with the name of the child 'author-to-be'.) Invite children to fill in the blanks, and illustrate their books, using their own ideas. Give unsure children a limited range of options from which to make their selection; for instance in the *Brown Bear, Brown Bear* example, suggest objects from around the classroom or the playground.

Sentence games

These activities can be useful for formative or summative assessment when children have completed a particular piece or stage of writing, or if you have been teaching them word- or sentence-level skills. Ask them, in groups or pairs, to design a game to display their own understanding, and to test their peers', of a particular writing feature on which they have been focusing. The children should write suitable sentences, e.g. on strips of paper, to form a 'pack' for use during the game, or else write separate words that could form sentences on cards. The object can be for players to point out where the selected writing feature appears – or should or could appear – in sentences. A reward will be needed for getting things right, e.g. advancing on the game board, or collecting toy treasure.

Some objects of different games could be:

- to make up two sentences that follow one after the other, and to show where the full stops and capital letters go;
- to show which word/s in a sentence need/s capital letters;
- to make up a sentence using a connective (players might gain higher rewards for connectives other than 'and', 'but', 'so' and 'then');
- to join two sentences together appropriately with a connective, thus forming a new, longer sentence;
- to decide which sentences need question marks (and/or exclamation marks);
- to make up questions and/or exclamations;
- to suggest an 'interesting' word to replace a 'boring' one in a sentence;
- to change a present-tense sentence into the past tense, e.g. using '-ed' endings for verbs; or
- to change words in a sentence, e.g. 'we done', 'they run', 'you was', 'catched' or 'swimmed', so that there is grammatical agreement, or so that verb tenses are accurate.

Fellow players, or a supervising adult, must agree that a child has succeeded and gained the 'reward' before the game can continue.

DIFFERENTIATION

Ensure that game designers and players are grouped according to their proficiency with the writing feature selected as the theme for their game.

Make-believe lists

This activity can form part of a unit of work on list writing, inspiring able writers while stimulating unconfident ones. Find a story text that the children know well in which a character or characters undertake any activity, e.g. cooking, shopping, a journey or a party, the preparations for which are not detailed in the text (Michael Rosen's *We're Going on a Bear Hunt* is just one of many). Ask children to write their own lists of items they imagine the character/s might find useful for the activity. Encourage them to use their imagination, though their lists must be as thorough as possible and 'fit' the story. Share and celebrate the most original ideas.

DIFFERENTIATION

Confident children should write while the less confident may draw each item on the list. Ask the latter to draw fairly small, and to set out each picture in list format, e.g. in columns, or one under the other. Having drawn each item, they may be happy to label the illustrations afterwards.

Critical thinking

We ask children to review, appraise and seek ways of improving their writing much of the time. The suggestions below highlight these activities.

Reviewing the process

The sub-sections below illustrate two versions of this approach.

The techniques and process of writing

Before children undertake a writing task, ask them to remain alert throughout as to how they are tackling it, and in what order. Afterwards, ask at least some of them to outline to you and/or their peers:

- what the task was, and who it was for (e.g. writing instructions on making a paper hat, for a younger child to take to a party);

- what they did, in what sequence (e.g. in this case maybe they planned the different parts of instruction writing with the teacher, ran through useful vocabulary and phrases with a talk partner, then wrote a title, introductory sentence, list of equipment, five instructions and a conclusion); and

- what features their writing has: for this, get them to use the 'metalanguage' (specialist terminology) of writing as much as possible (e.g. 'imperatives', 'present tense', 'bullet points', 'commas', 'full stops', 'time markers', 'connectives').

DIFFERENTIATION

Allow confident thinkers the freedom to describe the process as they wish. Give unsure children a few, limited choices of response, some appropriate, some less so, from which to choose.

The thought and planning processes

In addition, especially with confident writers, prime them to be aware while writing of:

- how they reacted to the task (e.g. immediately recalling other similar tasks, feeling unsure about some aspects, wondering where to start, coping well or otherwise with any decisions required);

- what they thought during the task (if they found some parts hard or easy, what they liked or disliked about the task, and how they resolved problems such as mistakes or unfamiliar words);

- what helped them during the task (e.g. talk with a partner, reference materials, recall of similar tasks); and

- their immediate feelings about the task at the end of the session (how well they think they have done, what they think they have learnt or wish they had done differently, and what they think are their writing strengths and weaknesses).

Ask at least some children to feed back to you and/or their peers on these aspects too.

Getting used to 'observing themselves at work' in this way, on a regular basis, heightens children's powers of metacognition (thinking about their learning).

DIFFERENTIATION

Invite children who are especially alert to their thought processes to represent them diagrammatically, perhaps in emoticons (facial symbols representing the emotions) alongside headings for different aspects of the task (e.g. 'List of equipment', 'Instructions', 'Special vocabulary', 'Punctuation', etc.); they can then explain these to the class.

Uncertain children, particularly children with recall problems, should summarise these processes *immediately* after they finish writing; alternatively, stop them at several points *during* the task, asking them what they have done and thought so far. Ask struggling thinkers closed questions, e.g. if they can't remember the task instanced above, ask whether it was a recount of how they made a hat, or instructions on making a hat; and whether it was for their parents, one of the seven dwarves or a party-going child. If they are unsure what they thought while writing, ask them, for example, whether they found remembering bullet points easy, or how they coped if they forgot some parts of the hat-making process.

Ringing the changes

As soon as they are writing texts of any length, children benefit from explicit demonstration of the various phases of the writing process: planning, drafting, revising, proofreading and presentation or 'publishing'. Beware of introducing these in such a way as to demotivate eager writers by giving the impression that, the more they write, the more you will give them to do! The approaches described in the following two sub-sections help, sustaining children's interest in their work.

Thoughtful displays

Space out the stages of the writing process on the timetable. For example, undertake a short block of work on planning a particular kind of writing one or more weeks in advance of the children writing it; only later, resurrect this work and ask children to write from it. Once children have written a text, leave another week or more before, with your coaching, they try revising or proofreading it, and, if a final 'neat' presentation is required – for instance, making the edited text up into books – leave a further time-lag before they do this. As a result, children will approach each stage with fresh vigour, and a more self-critical eye.

At the writing stage of the process, if children are writing at length and will later be editing their work, encourage them to write on alternate lines (shading the 'blank' ones faintly in pencil, or asking writers to do so, will help remind them). This gives them scope to add ideas or details, or to reorder sentences, during the revision phase.

At each separate stage of the writing process, before it begins, prepare the children for the fact that one outcome will be a display, explaining, celebrating and appraising their achievement. Thus:

- Mount a wall display (or do an interactive whiteboard presentation) of any materials generated during the planning phase: storyboards, notes, mind or concept maps, word lists, etc. (whether produced by you or the children). Invite the children to help you caption or label these. Captions must explain what is important about planning (i.e. that this is when a lot of 'work' in the form of thinking takes place); what each item of planning is; when and why it was done, and by whom; and why it was useful in the planning process. Encourage children to give their opinions (e.g. by voting, or adding comments in 'speech bubbles'): which items, notes, storyboard features, etc. are the most original, unusual, detailed, clearest, their favourite?

- At the writing (i.e. pre-corrected, drafting) stage, ask children to help you label a display of their work to explain what is important about drafting (i.e. that this is where a lot of 'thinking in the raw', including rethinking, takes place); and what the drafting process is (i.e. 'rough' writing, which may be 'untidy' and subject to change). Again, encourage children to give their opinions (by voting or captioning): which pieces of writing show the 'roughness' of the process best, are not afraid of taking risks, e.g. with spelling, or show adventurous changes from the planning stage?

- Showcase in some form the work of children capable of editing (e.g. of adding to and changing their drafts on alternate blank lines, as suggested above). Particularly confident writers may benefit from splitting this phase into two: first, revising (making substantive changes, such as the order of sentences, word choices, splitting text into paragraphs, adding phrases or sentences, introducing punctuation for effect, etc.) and second, proofreading (making 'secretarial' changes, such as amending lower-case or capital letters, punctuating for sense and spelling improvements). Ask them to comment, in captions or labels, on their reasons for the alterations they made, and how they ensured they were clear (e.g. by using arrows, a 'marking code', symbols, neat crossing-out, etc.).

Invite the children to vote, or comment in further captions, on changes they particularly like and why; and on the importance of the messy process of editing (it requires self-critical thinking – a much higher-level skill than neatness!).

- Sometimes highlight the place of presentation or 'publication' by displaying examples, also captioned. Remember though that 'publication' can take various forms, e.g. tape-recorded readings, readings of heavily amended, messy text, videoed presentations from a script, word-processed text, leaflets or books: it need not always be in the form of neat handwriting. Invite children to comment, in their labelling, on the limited 'thinking power' involved in this phase (which may simply consist of accurate copying). Ask them to vote on their favourite 'finished products', justifying their choices with reasons.

- Finally, occasionally undertake an overarching display of all these phases side by side – ideally illustrating the gestation and production of one writing task. For this, ensure that the children help provide an 'overview' of the whole process in headings and/or flow diagrams.

DIFFERENTIATION

An alternative method of display is to prepare a large board with jumbled headings ready for use: 'Planning', 'Drafting', 'Editing', 'Presentation'. Show the children captions that explain each phase, for instance for the heading 'Planning': 'At this stage our thinking can take many forms. We think very hard and make a lot of decisions but we can change these later if we like.' As a writing task progresses, ask children to match captions to headings; to suggest the sequence for the headings; and to locate where the various stages of their work should go under the appropriate headings. Ensure that less confident writers still have opportunities to gloss displayed items with their own opinions and comments: class votes suggested by you (e.g. favourite plan for a story ending, clearest mind map, most thorough editing job) will help to focus these.

Spot the difference

- Collect and display enlarged illustrations of authors' draft manuscripts, clearly demonstrating the messiness of the editorial process. Illustrated literary diaries and calendars provide a useful source; so too do facsimile editions of writers' texts (often held in large public libraries). You may be able to obtain reproductions of Beatrix Potter's from the V & A Museum, or Lewis Carroll's from the British Library, both in London; A. A. Milne's from Trinity College Library, Cambridge; or J. M. Barrie's play version of *Peter Pan* from the Beinecke Rare Book and Manuscript Library, Yale University. Incorporate these into your display about the revision stage of writing. Alternatively, show such illustrations to the children side by side with reproductions of the same passages of the authors' published texts (e.g. on an interactive board); invite them to 'spot the differences', for example by highlighting, circling or colour-coding the original words and the changes in the final text. Encourage debate: which authorial changes do the children feel are improvements? Why or why not?

- Over a school year, collect photocopies of your children's writing-in-progress: any planning on paper, first or incomplete drafts prior to editing, well-edited and final versions. Anonymise these and bank them in a useful format, e.g. as OHTs or scanned-in files. In subsequent years, use this resource: ask children to 'spot the difference' from one stage of a writing task to the next, or to supplement their 'thoughtful displays' with these examples; otherwise, introduce them as a prelude to work on editing or presentation.

- When children undertake a kind of writing they have done with you or colleagues before, collect together copies of their previous similar task. After they have drafted and polished their current work, give out their earlier pieces and invite them to compare the two. Ask them what they have learnt about undertaking this kind of writing from one task to the next; what they have learnt about writing in general; what they now do better; and how they have progressed as editors.

DIFFERENTIATION

Challenging children to 'find at least *x* differences' will help to focus the activity. Making 'spot the difference' tasks active and interactive, i.e. asking children to come out and mark up displayed text, will stimulate kinaesthetic learners. Ask those who need support not *why* they feel a 'difference' (i.e. an amendment) is an improvement or otherwise, but *what* it does to the original text that is better or worse.

Evaluations

Evaluation pervades most writing tasks in the form of marking, often by the teacher. The formats outlined in the two following sub-sections share out the task of critical thinking with the learner. Choose one or the other – ideally as a whole-school approach, adopted in every classroom (overall, the 'Critical friends' format works best with the majority of KS1 children).

Critical friends

Pair children up, if possible, based on their progress as writers, handwriters and spellers. (As much as possible, nominate partners who would not choose each other, while avoiding both close friendships and 'difficult' combinations.) It may work to use current pairings, e.g. existing talk or learning partners, however beware: children well-matched for some activities or areas of the curriculum are not necessarily so in others.

For any task in which there is to be a complete 'writing product', e.g., a plan or an edited text, a list of spellings being learnt or tested or a piece of handwriting practice, ask these pairs of critical friends to sit together. Nominate one in each pair as A, the other as B. Immediately after your teaching and the task, ask pairs to show each other their work. Invite A to show or read their output aloud and B to comment on it; then, after an appropriate amount of time, or at a signal from you, B can do the same and A can comment. For instance:

- In the planning of writing, set criteria on which they should remark. For example, if you model planning for a report (information) text and then ask children to do their own plans, you might pre-set as indicators of success (a) ideas for at least three sub-topics on the subject, and (b) a jotted list of useful vocabulary. Pairs can judge if each of them has met these criteria.

- During editing, also pre-set clear criteria for success. For example, on one piece of writing you might require the children (a) to add details to a description, and (b) to improve their punctuation. Partners can again exchange comments on these aspects.

- During spelling learning and practice, ask partners to test each other, e.g. by dictating sentences containing the 'target words' for spelling. Alternatively, they can check that each has recorded his/her target spellings several times correctly, for instance in a spelling log.

- In the course of handwriting practice, critical friends can judge each others' letter formation against any teacher modelling of posture, grip, paper position, letter shapes and movements. (In this case, partners should comment *while* handwriting is being done.)

Ensure that it is not the critical friend but the child whose work it is who undertakes any subsequent 'marking' and amendments. (They can use a different colour where appropriate, thus enabling you to judge their progress easily.) Praise children who use your criteria, advise each other sensitively, listen to their partners and act on their advice.

DIFFERENTIATION

Reward any especially mature self-critics by 'promoting them out' of this approach, allowing them instead to undertake detailed self-evaluation and marking, as outlined below. (It may help to give them a prompt sheet of aspects for improvement, as also listed below.)

The least confident self-critics can attach 'smiley' and 'glum' emoticon stickers to their texts to represent their perceived success or otherwise in writing tasks. As a development of this idea, record two or three criteria, e.g. at the end of their work or on the board – for instance 'How well I planned', 'Whether I used other connectives, not just "and" and "then" ' – and invite them to comment on these separately with 'smiley' or 'glum' stickers, or orally in class.

Self-evaluation

First, involve the children as a group in a critical appraisal of a displayed writing plan or text, for example an anonymised example of a child's work from a previous year, as suggested earlier. Invite volunteers to help you annotate it with suggested improvements. Always start by revising substantive aspects:

- layout;
- order of words or sentences;
- tedious or clumsy repetition of words, including connectives;
- amount of clarity and detail;
- appropriacy of vocabulary choices; and
- the use of punctuation and fonts for effect, e.g. an exclamation mark for surprise, block capitals for emphasis.

Together, use a different coloured pen or marker to improve each of these aspects. Stop after each kind of change (e.g. word and sentence order). Now ask writers independently to revise their texts in this one aspect (ideally in the same colour as you have), before you move on to demonstrate the next kind.

After this repeated process, examine proofreading changes: invite volunteers to help you improve the displayed text by amending – again in different colours:

- capital and lower case letters;
- punctuation for meaning and accuracy, e.g. full stops at the ends of sentences; and
- spellings.

Breaking down the editorial process into small steps in this way, alternating modelling with opportunities for individuals to make amendments to their own texts, helps them build editorial stamina, transfer their learning skills and progress effectively.

DIFFERENTIATION

This approach is best suited to an especially able class or group.

Affective thinking and emotional literacy

Ideas from earlier sections

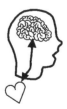

Many suggestions from earlier sections can contribute to affective thinking and emotional literacy: reminders of these are given in the sub-sections below.

Problem-solving

During mind-mapping in preparation for writing (see page 73), ensure that children contribute their own suggestions – personal memories, mnemonics, familiar tunes, lyrics and rhymes, factual recall, etc. – in order to consolidate their learning and understanding. This will boost self-esteem and help make the task personally meaningful.

The 'Making choices' approach (see page 77) highlights the uniqueness of every writer in a classroom, encouraging and legitimising children's willingness to 'be different'.

Creative thinking

Likewise, urging writers to 'Choose your own ...' (subject-matter, reader, text layout, etc.: see page 82) promotes risk-taking and the value of individuality.

Asking children 'How many kinds of writing ...?' (page 80) encourages them to be flexible and wide-ranging in their thinking – a quality some term 'fluency'.

For children with English as an additional language, inviting them to 'Imagine the words' to pictures in their first language (see page 83) recognises the importance of their linguistic and/or cultural backgrounds, and can help build a sense of self-worth.

Critical thinking

'Reviewing the process' of writing (see page 85) can help to develop intrapersonal abilities such as self-awareness and metacognitive reflection – as can self-evaluation (see page 90).

On the other hand, 'Critical friendships' between writers, handwriters and spellers (see page 89) can foster interpersonal skills: the sensitive handling of working relationships, mutual trust and respect, and the arts of negotiation and compromise. (Tactful support and constructive criticism are also required in working partnerships during the 'Transformations' approach in the 'Creative thinking' section: see page 82.)

Risk-taking

Openly discuss and value with writers, their ability and willingness to take risks; stress that risk-taking, i.e. trying unfamiliar things, is the only way learners learn. Challenge children sometimes to be 'brave enough' to make a choice or take a risk they would prefer not to. One approach is to designate the occasional writing session as a 'risk day'; alternatively, challenge unconfident children to go to a 'risk group' or 'risk table' to write at least once every week or fortnight. Some aspects of writing in which to encourage risk-taking are:

- spelling without aids or help;
- writing (i.e. drafting) without rubbers or erasers, crossing out neatly instead;
- writing from memory, without pictorial reminders, reference books or planners;
- tackling a blank piece of paper, e.g. writing without the support of 'sentence frames';
- using newly introduced vocabulary, time markers or connectives; and
- writing on a new topic, or for a new kind of reader.

DIFFERENTIATION

Such challenges can be confined, if desired, to certain writers only, able or otherwise.

Boosting independence in 'early finishers'

Sometimes writers complete a task both successfully and earlier than expected. Identify any children who do so on a regular basis; encourage them in such situations not to come to you but to choose one from a bank of generic 'follow-on tasks', explained briefly on laminated index cards in a box, placed somewhere accessible. These tasks should *not* involve 'writing more of the same', or, indeed, a great deal of extra writing, either of which will demotivate children from finishing their work in the first place! Typical tasks (apart from proceeding to edit the text with a partner: see page 89) can be:

- If you could only save three words/phrases/lines/sentences from your writing, which would they be? Mark them in some way, e.g. a colour or a smiley face. If you like, write down what you like about each one.

- Do a diagram of how you felt and thought about your writing as you were doing it. Show at least three stages.

- Look at the way the teacher has marked your last three pieces of work. Write three messages, answering him/her.

- Draw your face with a speech bubble beside the mouth. In the bubble, give advice about how to do this kind of writing.

This approach will foster 'early finishers'' independence of action and 'learning stamina', while also helping them think about their writing.

DIFFERENTIATION

Such ideas are appropriate only for able writers who genuinely have successfully completed earlier writing tasks.

Slotting approaches together

Many of the approaches described under 'Problem-solving', 'Creative thinking' and 'Critical thinking' – and in this section too – can be 'slotted together' to create an extended block of work if desired. Each phase should take children's thinking about their writing to a new level. This in-depth approach will also help them develop 'learning stamina'.

Questioning skills

Using texts as models

To develop question writing (plus question mark punctuation), start by reading and discussing a text that is largely structured around questioning. You can then use this as a model for the children's writing. Examples, especially in fiction and poetry, abound. *Who's Making that Mess?*, by Phillip Hawthorn and Jenny Taylor, is a flap-book that can provide inspiration for 'Who's?' questioning in writing on a somewhat different theme, e.g., 'Who's Making that Noise/Building that House/ Swimming like That?', etc. Jane Yolen's *How Do Dinosaurs Say Goodnight?* can support the composition of 'How?' and 'Do?' questions, e.g. about dragons, fairies or aliens instead of dinosaurs. *What's the Time, Mr Wolf?*, Colin Hawkins' simple picture book, can inspire books made by the children showcasing the 'What's the?' formula, e.g. 'What's the Matter/Weather/Day/Season, Mr/Mrs Shark/Hedgehog/ Pig/Cat?' Jo Brown's *Where's My Mummy?* provides a framework of 'Are you?' and 'Can you?' questions, so can also lead to writing on other themes, e.g. 'Where's My Ball/Teacher/Pet?'

In poetry, W. B. Yeats' one question in the short poem *To a Squirrel at Kyle-Na-No*, 'Why should you run/Through the shaking tree/As though I'd a gun?', can spark 'Why should you?' poems. Ask children to think what is unexpected or special in the behaviour of other animals, e.g. ducks feed with only their tails showing. They can then construct poems beginning 'Why?', including suggestions of possible reasons for this behaviour beginning with 'As though'. Roger McGough's *Shark*, asking 'Ever see?' a shark doing something ludicrous, provides a humorous, and simpler, starting point. It can result in 'Ever see?' poems about other creatures or people doing ridiculous things, followed by advice on how to react if we should witness them.

DIFFERENTIATION

Able thinker-writers should not need the question framework you have provided, as suggested above; insist they use more challenging question words, e.g. 'How?', 'Why?', 'What?' or 'What if?' – or even devise their own question formats. If the types of text mentioned above are too simple, give more able question writers different, more demanding text models. The 'Is it true that . . .?' questioning in Robert Munsch's *The Paper Bag Princess* provides a challenging framework for quest-like tales about other characters; the *Young Puzzle Adventures* series published by Usborne – illustrated with mazes, maps and more, setting readers problems and mysteries to solve and asking many questions, such as 'How does [a particular character] know?', 'Which island?' and 'Can you find a way?' – can inspire children to devise their own puzzle books, frequently questioning the reader.

Questioning the curriculum

Your announcement of a new topic or unit of work is an opportunity to ask children to write questions related to the subject, informing you of facts or concepts they do not, as yet, know or understand. Giving them a stimulus before they write, e.g. showing an artefact or illustrations connected with the topic, or playing a relevant sound recording, can help prompt appropriate questions. So, too, can brainstorming or mind/concept-mapping everything the children *do* know as a class or group. Record and display this list or diagram: it will help the children perceive the gaps in their knowledge and understanding. Now encourage them to write outstanding queries, in question format if they can. (Show them examples, e.g. 'I can't remember where speech marks go' can be reworded as 'Where do you put speech marks?'; 'I don't know about Easter' can become 'What happens at Easter?', or 'Why do we celebrate it?') If possible, once you have the children's written questions, display them alongside your planning, also on view in some enlarged, simple format; by cross-referencing to this, point out where you will try to ensure opportunities to answer their questions or explore them. Ideally, return to the children's questions (which you can bank) at the end of the block of work. Together, decide which have been answered or explored, and if any remain unresolved, discuss why that is.

Bring the work to a close at the end of the unit or topic by inviting each child to record a statement beginning 'I would still like to know/I am still not sure/I still don't understand . . .' (If you wish, encourage them to convert these statements into questions. They can even write these up as questioning letters or emails to an expert or a character connected with the topic, e.g., a nurse who has visited, or the Victorian headteacher of their school; if so, ensure that the writers receive replies, real or concocted!) Aim to convey that learning is a continuous, never-ending process: there is always more to know and understand. (At the same time, find some way for learners to pursue their unanswered questions further if they are keen to, e.g. via self-designed projects for homework, to be shared later with peers in class.)

DIFFERENTIATION

Challenge the really keen and curious writers to devise the most unusual and interesting questions they can, i.e. questions that no one else is likely to think of. Celebrate the most imaginative, e.g. in a class vote. Ensure that they have the opportunity to research these, for example out of school, and to share their findings in due course with their peers. Give unsure writers copies of just one or two writing frames for their questions, e.g. 'How does/do?', 'What is/are/was/were?' Ensure they realise that they *do* already have knowledge and understanding via the brainstorming/concept-mapping exercise above (for instance, on probing them they may recognise that they know Easter is a festival, without remembering what it celebrates).

PLAN-DO-REVIEW FORMATS: A CASE STUDY

The following example of Writing activity was incorporated in a unit of work at Year 2 around instruction writing. The work aimed to develop questioning skills, problem-solving, creative thinking and critical thinking; for some writers, it also encouraged affective thinking and emotional literacy. Lessons followed the sequence of 'plan-do-review', similar to that promoted by Belle Wallace in her TASC problem-solving wheel (see Introduction, page 4).

Invitation writing

Different children were made aware of the specific learning outcomes I expected from them, as described here.

Learning objectives: All children to write invitations incorporating at least two instructions (what to bring and/or wear, and/or when to come, etc.); all to choose freely an appropriate event as the subject of their invitation (creative thinking); some to group and sequence their ideas into two or three different components of the invitation (problem-solving) – information, instructions and persuasive text; some to choose between two layouts for the invitation, and between the teacher's pen-pal and their own as the audience (problem-solving); and a few to make the free choice of an appropriate audience (thus making an affective connection with the task), also selecting their own – indirectly persuasive – words and phrases, e.g. 'brilliant', 'delicious', 'beautiful', 'exciting' (creative thinking); the most sensitive thinkers to suit their persuasive phraseology precisely to their selected reader (emotional literacy).

The first lesson: analysis (problem-solving)

For three lessons previously the children in this class had read, used and written simple instructions, in conjunction with cookery activities. All had grasped that many instructions need a list of equipment or materials, and a large number could explain that instructions often consist of several 'bossy' sentences (as we described them), whose sequencing needs careful consideration. For homework I now asked them to collect and bring in examples of invitations; I, too, had samples.

This first lesson, I explained that we would soon be writing invitations. I announced without preamble that 'Invitations are a bit like instructions', writing this statement on the board. We then passed round, displayed and read out as many invitations as we could, including those from *Angelina Ballerina's Invitation to the Ballet* by Katharine Holabird, which differed widely in style and tone. I modelled a 'pondering mode' during this phase, frowning thoughtfully, and repeatedly and silently pointing to the statement on display. During group/guided reading, pairs studied an example of an invitation and an example of instructions, of appropriate readability levels, side by side. I asked them to search for similarities (problem-solving). (Struggling readers compared their design and layout; struggling thinkers had examples they already knew well.) I urged them then to devise a statement or question resulting from their comparisons. Circulating, I suggested sentence/question frames for the less confident, e.g. 'Instructions are/have . . ., and invitations are/have too', or 'Where is/are the . . . in an invitation?'; I urged the most able thinkers to devise questions only, incorporating a word such as 'instructions', 'lists', 'order', 'information' or 'persuade' (the latter concept understood by a few). For these they could use frames such as 'How is/are?', 'What kind of?', 'Where?', etc.

In the plenary, we returned to my statement on the board. Acting as chair, I invited pairs to announce their statement or question. After each, refraining from comment, I sought out further statements or questions that the children felt endorsed, added to or, indeed, contradicted those just made, e.g. by asking 'Who has a statement/question a bit like/very unlike that one?' I also invited them to comment on each other's ideas as they were stated, or to answer the questions posed. Through this discussion-cum-question session, their thinking about invitations developed considerably. Statements included 'Instructions have writing on separate lines, and invitations have writing on separate lines as well', and 'They both want you to do something'; high-level ideas included 'Instructions are mostly to boss you around, but invitations do other things as well'; and the children's thought-provoking questions included 'How bossy can you be in an invitation?' and 'Can you say "Please" in instructions?' Most children now saw that invitations were, partly, instructions in 'polite disguise'; that, like instructions, they often included lists of items (things to bring or wear), though not usually in list format or layout; that, like some instructions, they incorporated information (in their case contact details, date, time, place and occasion); and that both types of text could 'make you do things', whether through pleading, threatening, instructing or attracting the reader. A few also recognised that the order of sentences was important: some sentences, grouped together, described the occasion, while others, also grouped together, gave polite instructions, and yet more might make the event sound unmissable! I praised the class for its work: although they had written nothing yet, they had produced a mass of ideas (which I had recorded). I stressed that the 'work' had been in these, the talk and the comparisons.

The second lesson: choices, and writing begins (creative thinking and problem-solving)

Next lesson, I showed the class a photograph of my seven-year-old Sri Lankan pen-pal, plus a drawing and letter he had sent me describing the country's Buddhist New Moon festival, and wishing I could come. I suggested that he would love the children to come too, and asked if they would like to write back, inviting him to some forthcoming local event or celebration. Numerous children in class revealed that they too had pen-pals or distant friends. I saw the opportunity for choice-making (i.e. problem-solving) here, and for ensuring children made an affective connection with the task: I invited everyone to select either my pen-pal, or one of their own, as their intended reader. The children were motivated by the opportunity to make their own choices; I also gave them free choice of event, whereupon they rapidly settled on upcoming occasions such as birthday parties, Easter egg hunts, camping trips and more (creative thinking).

We now 'graphic-mapped' on the interactive board two styles of invitation layout: centred, and justified left (i.e. representing the text in lines, not words, like the text alignment icons on any computer word-processing toolbar). I asked all writers to choose one or other style. I also displayed an enlarged translation of my pen-pal's invitation. We read this together; at my request, three willing helpers located and colour-coded three distinct aspects of the text: information about the event and the sender's contact details, instructions on what to bring and wear, and alluring words, phrases and descriptions to persuade the reader to attend. From this exercise, many children perceived that the first two aspects were separately grouped, while persuasive phraseology occurred throughout.

I reminded the children that they had chosen specific readers, occasions and text layouts, and they now began writing their invitations. All were urged to include detailed information *and* instructions, as my pen-pal's model text had done; more able writers were reminded of the need to use 'alluring' phraseology, and to group the informative and instructional parts of the text separately. I asked emotionally astute thinkers to consider their readers carefully: what words and phrases would most likely persuade them to come? What kinds of food or entertainment did they like? Did they like excitement, surprises, games? Might they need reassurance about what to wear or bring or what might happen at the occasion?

The lesson culminated with a game. I asked children to read out selected words and phrases written so far; the class was challenged to guess from these either the occasion of the invitation or (with more able writers) the personality, likes or dislikes of the guest being invited (problem-solving).

The third lesson: into critical thinking

I began by showing the children an anonymised example of a child's invitation. On the interactive board I had jumbled the sentences – each 'boxed' – so that their order was illogical (instructions, information and persuasive sentences randomly mixed). Volunteers came to the front and helped me to drag these into a more sensible order, for example grouping time, place and venue together, and persuasive description just before the contact details (problem-solving and critical thinking).

In light of this exercise, each child now reviewed their writing-in-progress with an ability-matched 'critical friend'. I urged partners to help each other number any sentences they had already written into a more logical sequence (critical thinking). We heard readings of some children's previous and revised sequences; I praised any writers who had made changes for showing powers of critical thinking.

Children proceeded to complete their invitation writing. Circulating, I continued to remind all writers of the need for a consistent layout and persuasive phraseology, and the most mature thinkers to try to tailor this phraseology precisely to their readers' personalities. At the end of the lesson, I issued everyone with cards in three colours: red for information text, blue for instruction text and yellow for persuasive words and sentences. During readings of the invitations aloud by some writers, the audience had to hold up the appropriate card when they heard the corresponding kind of text. This was a useful instant assessment of their understanding of the different aspects of invitations; it also enabled the children sitting together listening to perceive whether ideas in a text had been grouped well and logically. After each reading, I asked the class to score the piece of writing out of five, by a show of hands, for its logical grouping of sentences (if they had kept the same coloured card aloft in response to at least two consecutive sentences or ideas, the grouping was likely to be quite sensible!). When listening to more able writers, I asked the audience to count how many persuasive words and phrases they heard used; writers had to tell the class what would appeal to their chosen readers about their word choices. These activities, as I explained to the children, were exercises in critical thinking: deciding what did or did not work in a text.

The three invitations in Figure 3.4 vary in their ability to organise different aspects of the text: Rebecca's is particularly logical. Both Sam and Abby

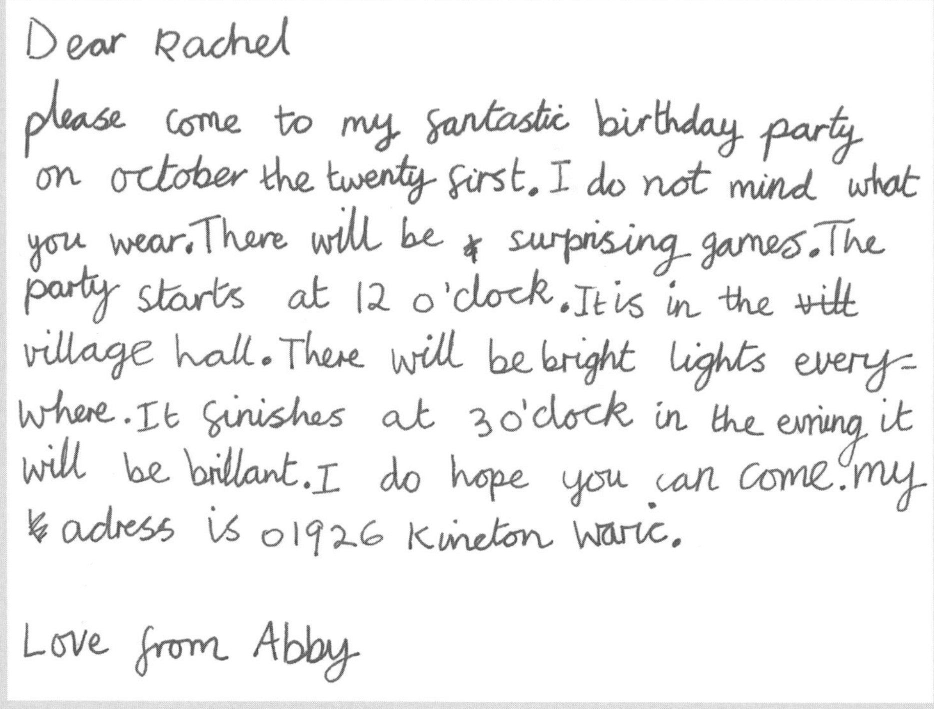

> Dear Rachel
>
> please come to my fantastic birthday party on october the twenty first. I do not mind what you wear. There will be surprising games. The party starts at 12 o'clock. It is in the village hall. There will be bright lights everywhere. It finishes at 3 o'clock in the evning it will be brillant. I do hope you can come. my adress is 01926 Kineton Warc.
>
> Love from Abby

Figure 3.4a Invitation to a birthday party

demonstrate consideration of their reader ('I do not mind what you wear', 'well mayby not you, luici because you're a girl'). Each writer has chosen one of two layouts and sustained it (problem-solving); they have each used creative thinking in their choice of event and/or of appropriate persuasive language.

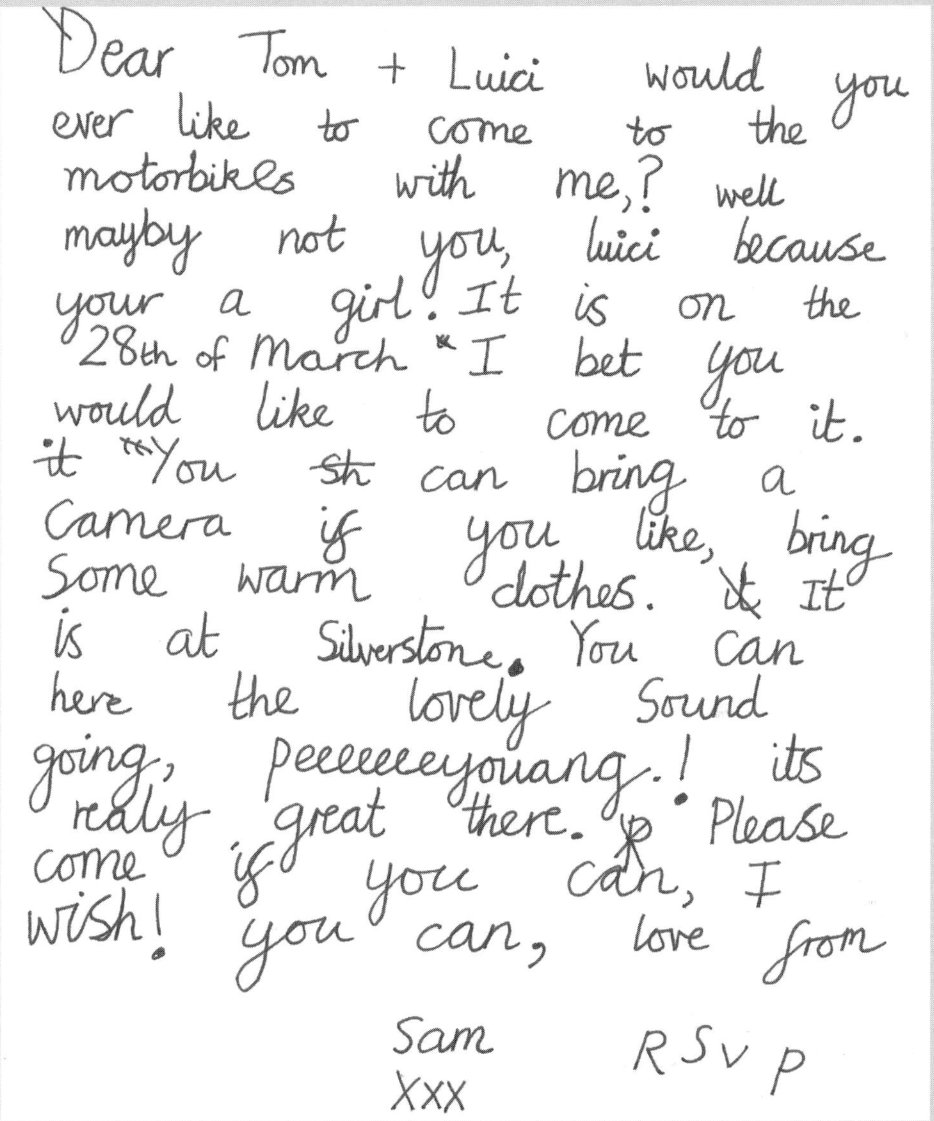

Dear Tom + Luici would you ever like to come to the motorbikes with me,? well mayby not you, luici because your a girl! It is on the 28th of March "I bet you would like to come to it. it "You sth can bring a Camera if you like, bring some warm clothes. It It is at Silverstone. You can here the lovely Sound going, Peeeeeeyouang.! its realy great there. Please come if you can, I wish! you can, love from

Sam   RSVP
Xxx

Figure 3.4b Invitation to Silverstone

Dear Delaney,

Please come to my Easter party,

4 oclock to 9oclock the next day.
Easter Saterday to Easter Sunday. (we myet have an
egghunt.) My Adress is England Kineton Warwickshire
banbury Road Rose House. You can dress up like a
bunny or an easter egg x but don,t get dirty!

you can take your sleeping bag if you want to.
please come of you will miss the fun.

from Rebecca.

RSVp

Figure 3.4c Invitation to an Easter party

Further reading, contacts and resources

Antidote (2004) *The Emotional Literacy Handbook*. London: David Fulton Publishers.

Bailey, T. (1987) *Instrumental Enrichment and Cross-curricular Bridging: A Handbook of Suggestions*. London: London Borough of Enfield.

Bearne, E. (2002) *Making Progress in Writing*. London: RoutledgeFalmer.

Blagg, N. *et al.* (1988) *Somerset Thinking Skills Course*. Oxford: Blackwell.

Bloom, B. S. (1956) *Taxonomy of Educational Objectives*. Boston, MA: Allyn and Bacon.

de Bono, E. (1970) *Lateral Thinking*. London: BBC Books.

de Bono, E. (1976) *Teaching Thinking*. London: Penguin Books.

de Bono, E. (1992) *Teach your Child to Think*. London: Penguin Books.

de Bono, E. (2000) *Six Thinking Hats®*. London: Penguin Books.

Bowkett, S. (1997) *Imagine That . . .: A Handbook of Creative Learning Activities for the Classroom*. Stafford: Network Educational Press.

Brown, G. and Wragg, E. C. (2001) *Questioning in the Primary School*. London: RoutledgeFalmer.

Burden, R. and Williams, M. (eds.) (1998) *Thinking through the Curriculum*. London: Routledge.

Buzan, T. (2000) *The Mind Map Book*. London: BBC Worldwide Ltd.

Buzan, T. (2002) *How to Mind Map*. London: Thorsons.

Claxton, G. (1997) *Hare Brain Tortoise Mind: Why Intelligence Increases when you Think Less*. London: Fourth Estate.

Claxton, G. and Lucas, B. (2004) *Be Creative: Essential Steps to Revitalize your Work and Life*. London: BBC Books.

Costello, P. J. M. (2000) *Thinking Skills and Early Childhood Education*. London: David Fulton Publishers.

Craft, A. (2003) *Creativity across the Primary Curriculum: Framing and Developing Practice*. London: Routledge.

Dean, G. (1999) *The National Literacy Strategy: Supporting and Challenging More Able Pupils in the Literacy Hour*. Cambridge: Cambridgeshire School Improvement Programme, Advisory Service.

Dean, G. (2001) *Challenging the More Able Language User, 2nd edition*. London: David Fulton Publishers.

DfEE (2000) *National Literacy and Numeracy Strategies: Guidance on Teaching Able Children*. Ref: LNGT.

Early Vision Ltd. (2004) *Let's Play and Learn* (video and audio CD theme packs about working and everyday life). Ross-on-Wye: Early Vision Ltd.

Eyre, D. (1997) *Able Children in Ordinary Schools*. London: David Fulton Publishers.

Eyre, D. and McClure, L. (2001) *Curriculum Provision for the Gifted and Talented in the Primary School: English, Maths, Science and IT*. London: David Fulton Publishers.

Feldhusen, J. F. (2002) 'Creativity: the knowledge base and children', *High Ability Studies*, 13: 2.

Feldhusen, J. F. (2003) 'Reflections on the development of creative achievement', *Gifted and Talented International*, 18: 1.

Feuerstein, R. (1980) *Instrumental Enrichment: An Intervention Program for Cognitive Modifiability*. Baltimore, MD: University Park Press.

Fisher, R. (1990) *Teaching Children to Think*. Oxford: Blackwell.

Fisher, R. (1995) *Teaching Children to Learn*. Cheltenham: Stanley Thornes.

Fisher, R. (1999) *First Stories for Thinking*. Oxford: Nash Pollock Publishing.

Fisher, R. (2000) *First Poems for Thinking*. Oxford: Nash Pollock Publishing.

Fisher, R. (2003) *Teaching Thinking: Philosophical Enquiry in the Classroom, 2nd edition*. London: Continuum.

Gardner, H. (1983) *Frames of Mind*. London: Fontana Press.

Gardner, H. (1993) *Multiple Intelligences: The Theory in Practice*. Oxford: Basic Books.

Gardner, H. (2000) *Intelligence Reframed*. Oxford: Basic Books.

Gardner, H. (2001) *Good Work: When Excellence and Ethics Meet*. Oxford: Basic Books.

Gilhooey, K. J. (1996) *Thinking, Directed, Undirected and Creative*. London: Academic Press.

Goleman, D. (2004) *Emotional Intelligence, and Working with Emotional Intelligence* (omnibus edition). London: Bloomsbury.

Goodwin, P. (2004) *Literacy through Creativity*. London: David Fulton Publishers.

Green, M. (2002) *English for the More Able 1 (Ages 5–6)* (photocopiable task sheets). Dunstable: Folens Publishers.

Green, M. (2002) *English for the More Able 2 (Ages 6–7)* (photocopiable task sheets). Dunstable: Folens Publishers.

Hackman, S. (1998) *Able Children in the Literacy Hour*. Reading: National Centre for Literacy.

Hackman, S. (2004) *Fast Forward Level 3 to Level 4, 2nd edition* (interactive problem-solving literacy activities). London: Hodder and Stoughton.

Henshaw, C. (2004) *Thinking out of the Box* (a box of thinking-task cards). Cheltenham: Nijen Ltd, tel: 01242 57535.

Henshaw, C. (2004) *Emotional Intelligence out of the Box* (a box of affective-thinking task cards). Cheltenham: Nijen Ltd, tel: 01242 57535.

Higgins, S., Baumfield, V. and Leat, D. (eds) (2001) *Thinking through Primary Teaching*. London: Chris Kington Publishing.

Jeffers, M. and Hancock, T. (2004) *Thinking Skills: A Teacher's Guide*. Corsham: Hopscotch Educational Publishing.

Jones, J. (2004) 'The Emotionally Literate School', paper delivered at Headteachers' Conference, 'Celebrating Innovation and Creativity'. Bournemouth. March.

Jones, R. and Wyse, D. (2004) *Creativity in the Primary Curriculum*. London: David Fulton Publishers.

Kerry, T. L. (2002) *Mastering Teacher Skills: Questioning and Explaining in the Classroom*. London: Nelson Thornes.

Krathwohl, D., Masia, B. B. and Bloom, B. S. (1965) *Affective Domain: The Classification of Educational Goals (Taxonomy of Educational Objectives)*. Harlow: Longman Schools Division.

Lake, M. and Needham, M. (2000) *Top Ten Thinking Tactics: A Practical Introduction to the Thinking Skills Revolution*. Birmingham: Questions Publishing Co. Ltd.

Leyden, S. (2002) *Supporting the Child of Exceptional Ability, 3rd edition*. London: David Fulton Publishers.

Lipman, M. (1991) *Thinking in Education*. Cambridge: Cambridge University Press.

Longman Primary, *The Longman Book Project series* (non-fiction texts differentiated into 'tiered texts' within each book, thus spanning a range of reading abilities). Harlow: Longman.

Moses, B. (2001) *I feel Angry, I feel Sad, I feel Jealous* and *I feel Frightened* (illustrated books for children, *Our Emotions series*). London: Hodder Wayland.

Murris, K. n.d. *Storywise: Thinking through Stories.* n.p: Dialogue Works.

National Association of Head Teachers (2004) *Emotional Intelligence and Emotional Literacy*, Primary Leadership Paper 12. Haywards Heath: National Association of Head Teachers.

National Curriculum in Action (2004) *Creativity*, at *www.ncaction.org.uk/creativity*

Nolan, V. (ed.)(2000) *Creative Education: Educating a Nation of Innovators.* Stoke Manderville: Synectics Education Initiative.

Primary National Strategy/DfES (2004) 'Planning for gifted and talented children', in *Excellence and Enjoyment: Learning and Teaching in the Primary Years: Designing Opportunities for Learning.* London: DfES. Ref: DfES 0520–2004 G.

Primary National Strategy/DfES (2004) 'Developing peer and self-assessment', 'Involving children in
self-evaluation' and 'Marking partnerships', in *Excellence and Enjoyment: Learning and Teaching in the Primary Years: Assessment for Learning.* London: DfES. Ref: 0521–2004 G.

Primary National Strategy/DfES (2004) 'Independent and individual learning contexts', in *Excellence and Enjoyment: Learning and Teaching in the Primary Years: Classroom Community, Collaborative and Personalised Learning.* London: DfES. Ref: DfES 0522–2004 G.

Primary National Strategy/DfES (2004) 'Enquiry', 'Problem solving', 'Creative thinking', 'Information processing', 'Reasoning', 'Evaluation', 'Self-awareness', 'Managing feelings', 'Empathy' and 'Social skills', in *Excellence and Enjoyment: Learning and Teaching in the Primary Years: Learning to Learn: Progression in Key Aspects of Learning.* London: DfES. Ref: DfES 0524–2004 G.

QCA (2001) *Working with Gifted and Talented Children: Key Stages 1 and 2 English and Mathematics* (handbook, booklet of written examples and video). Sudbury: QCA. Refs: QCA/01/801 and 802.

QCA (2004) *Creativity: Find it, Promote it – Promoting Pupils' Creative Thinking and Behaviour across the Curriculum at Key Stages 1, 2 and 3.* Sudbury: QCA. Refs: QCA/04/1292.

Research Centre for Experiential Education (2004) *Being Yourself: A Box Full of Feelings* (an activity set of masks, cards, etc. for children between the ages of 2 and 7). Dover: Smallwood Publishing Ltd.

Rubery, P. (2004) Section on emotional literacy, in *From Lost Learning Opportunities to Drivers of Attainment.* Nottingham: National College for School Leadership.

Sharp, P. (2001) *Nurturing Emotional Literacy.* London: David Fulton Publishers.

Storyworlds Bridges series (reading books for more able KS1 readers, with guided reading cards and teaching guide). Oxford: Ginn Heinemann.

Teaching Think!ng Magazine, from Imaginative Minds Ltd/Questions Publishing Company Ltd, Birmingham tel: 0121 666 7878, *www.teachthinking.com*

Treetops All Stars series (reading books for more able KS1 readers at three differentiated levels, with teaching notes on activities and questioning). Oxford: Oxford University Press.

Wallace, B. (2000) *Teaching the Very Able Child.* London: David Fulton Publishers.

Wallace, B. (2001) *Teaching Thinking Skills Across the Primary Curriculum.* London: David Fulton Publishers.

Wallace, B. (2002) *Teaching Thinking Skills Across the Early Years.* London: David Fulton Publishers.

Wallace, B., Maker, J., Cave, D. and Chandler, S. (2004) *Thinking Skills and Problem-Solving: An Inclusive Approach.* London: David Fulton Publishers.

Useful websites

Antidote: Campaign for emotional Literacy: *www.antidote.org.uk*

'Blogging' software, allowing children to 'post' their writing online: *www.blogger.com*

Book reviews from children: *www.kidsreview.org.uk* (access on subscription)

Buzan Centres: *www.mind-map.com/index.htm*

Centre for Applied Emotional Intelligence: *www.emotionalintelligence.co.uk*

Concept-mapping software (no SMART board needed): SMART Ideas 3.1 at *www.smart-board.co.uk* and *education@smartboard.co.uk*

DfES guidance on 'gifted and talented' pupils: *www.standards.dfes.gov.uk/excellence/gift*

DfES literacy plans: *www.standards.dfes.gov.uk*

DfES thinking skills guidance:
www.standards.dfes.gov.uk/thinkingskills/guidance/567257?view=get

Emotional intelligence: Ei (UK) Limited: *www.eiuk.com*

Excellence in Cities website on the 'gifted and talented', accessible even outside Excellence in Cities areas: *www.brookes.ac.uk/go/cpdgifted*

Fisher, R. website at *www.teachingthinking.net*

'Internet trails': *www.mape.org.uk/activities*

Metacognition and learning how to learn: *www.learntolearn.org* and *www.acceleratedlearning.com*

Mind Manager (licensed software): *www.m-urge.com*; *www.minmanager.co.uk*

National Academy for Gifted and Talented Youth (NAGTY): *www.warwick.ac.uk/gifted*

National Association for Able Children in Education (NACE): *www.nace.co.uk*

Paths (Promoting Alternative Thinking Strategies: an emotional literacy programme): *www.channing-bete.com/positiveyouth/pages/paths/paths.html* or *http://modelprograms.samhsa.gov.pdfs/factsheets/paths.pdf*

QCA guidance on 'gifted and talented' pupils: *www.nc.uk.net/gt*

QCA optional extension/assessment tasks in English for more able pupils: *www.qca.org.uk/ages3–14/tests_tasks*

Richard Marsden's Museum Mind Map: *www.walsallgfl.org.uk*

School of Emotional Literacy: *www.schoolofemotional-literacy.com*

Stories from children: *www.creativewriting4kids.com* (access on subscription)

The Sustainable Thinking Classrooms programme, working with children in primary schools in Ulster: *www.sustainablethinking-classrooms.qub.ac.uk*

Teaching ideas (by subject, including literacy): *www.teachingideas.uk*

Teaching plans and resources for literacy: *www.literacymatters.com* and *www.hamilton-trust.org.uk*

Visual Mind (licensed software): *www.visual-mind.com/MindMapdownload.htm*

Writing from children: Kids on the Net at *http://kotn.ntu.ac.uk* and *Young Writer* magazine plus website at *www.youngwriter.org*

Please note that the author and publishers cannot guarantee that the above information, particularly about websites, will remain current.

Index